Secure World Foundation

Handbook for
New Actors in Space

Edited by Christopher D. Johnson

ISBN - 978-0-692-85141-8

TABLE OF CONTENTS

CHAPTER ONE:

ABOUT THE SECURE WORLD FOUNDATION

The Secure World Foundation envisions the secure, sustainable, and peaceful uses of outer space contributing to global stability on Earth. We work with governments, industry, international organizations, and civil society to develop and promote ideas and actions for international collaborations that achieve the secure, sustainable, and peaceful uses of outer space.

www.swfound.org

ACKNOWLEDGMENTS

The Secure World Foundation was assisted by many experts from governments, space agencies, private industry, and academia in the drafting of this document. This document reflects the position and views of the Secure World Foundation, and not those of the experts consulted. While all errors or omissions are entirely our fault, we are deeply grateful to the following individuals for their views and input.

First Workshop Participants
P.J. Blount, Dennis Burnett, Matt Duncan, Andrew D'Uva, Stephen Earle, Michael Gleason, Henry Hertzfeld, Karl Kensinger, Rich Leshner, Peter Marquez, Steve Mirmina, Clay Mowry, Mark Mulholland, Myland Pride, Ben Reed, Franceska Schroeder, Glenn Tallia, Gary Thatcher, and Jessica Young.

Second Workshop Participants
Kahina Aoudia, Paul Frakes, Talal Al Kaissi, Jonathan Garon, Rich Leshner, Mike Lindsay, Philippe Moreels, Nobu Okada, Kevin Pomfret, Rajeswari Rajagopalan, and Kazuto Suzuki.

External Experts
Laura Delgado López, Matt Duncan, Andrea Harrington, T.S. Kelso, Tanja Masson-Zwaan, T.J. Mathieson, Gerald Oberst, Mazlan Othman, Greg Wyler, and Satellite Associates.

Michael K. Simpson, PhD
Executive Director
Secure World Foundation

FOREWORD

Driven by Cold War tensions between the US and the Soviet Union, the space race began almost 60 years ago. Each power was racing to accomplish new feats in space and demonstrate its superiority. In 2017, while much remains the same, much has changed. Space actors comprise a wide variety of national and non-governmental entities comprising diverse rationales, goals, and activities. More than 70 states, commercial companies, and international organizations currently operate more than 1,500 satellites in Earth orbit. Driven largely by the commoditization of space technology and the lowering of barriers to participation, the number of space actors is growing.

This broadening of space has both advantages and disadvantages. On the positive side, it is leading to greatly increased technological innovations, lower costs, and greater access to the beneficial capabilities and services offered by satellites. However, the accelerated growth in space activities and the influx of new actors has the potential to exacerbate many of the current threats to the long-term sustainable use of space. These threats include on-orbit crowding, radio-frequency interference, and the chances of an incident in space sparking or escalating geopolitical tensions on Earth.

Will the growing number of new actors in space destabilize the space environment, creating new tensions between nations? Can the peaceful broadening of space allow a flourishing of inventiveness and industry? As new actors "join the club," they should consider the following questions:

What is the international and national legal framework that governs their space activities?

What governmental authorities will be regulating them?

What rights and responsibilities do they have in space?

What potential liabilities do they risk for their space activities?

How do governments provide oversight of private-sector space activities?

What is the purpose and the value of national space policy?

What mechanisms are there for coordinating national space activities among different agencies and entities?

What are the standard operating procedures for owners and operators in their chosen orbits?

The Secure World Foundation is proud to present this Handbook for New Actors in Space. It is intended to reach two categories of new actors: national governments beginning to develop national space policies and regulations, and start-up companies, universities, and all other non-governmental entities beginning their first forays into space activities.

The goal of this handbook is to provide new actors with a broad overview of the fundamental principles, laws, norms, and best practices for peaceful, safe, and responsible activities in space. Only a pragmatic and cooperative approach to space can ensure that all countries and peoples can derive the many benefits that space activities have to offer.

HOW TO USE THIS BOOK

This handbook is structured in three main chapters. Though meant to complement each other for a broad understanding of the entire scope of concern to new actors, certain chapters and sections will be of heightened interest to readers depending on their own expected space activity and the role that they will be playing in that activity.

Chapter One deals with the international legal and political order applicable to space activities, and gives an introduction to the most important and relevant topics in international space law and how they apply to states.

Chapter Two discusses how national space policy and national regulation apply to space, beginning with rationales for developing space policy and discussing in particular how to broadcast goals internationally and give guidance domestically. The chapter also includes a discussion of the common aspects of national space legislation. Because national governments are directly responsible for their national space activities, including the activities of non-governmental entities such as corporations and universities, national space policy and regulation are very important for both governments and individual space projects to understand. Governments initiating their space capabilities or drafting their space policies would be well served with an understanding of Chapter Two.

Chapter Three addresses responsible space operations, and provides an overview of the process from pre-launch frequency selections and coordination to payload review, launch services agreements between launch providers and operators, and mission and post-mission concerns. More technical than Chapters One or Two, this final chapter explores the operational side of space activities, and may be the chapter most consulted by new operators in space once they've familiarized themselves with the preceding chapters on international and national space law and policy.

Last, while textbooks on any of the various topics discussed in this book run into many hundreds of pages, this book aims to be both concise and readable. Rather than an exhaustive compendium of every facet and nuance of this incredibly rich field, this commentary is broad and comprehensive but contains only the most fundamental principles and topics.

Tanja Masson-Zwaan
President Emerita

International Institute
of Space Law

INTRODUCTION

Space is changing. The barriers to access to space are decreasing. Shrinking costs, less infrastructure, and lower technological hurdles all make space activities available to more people. Meanwhile, smaller programs with fewer necessary personnel enable more states and entities to participate in space projects. Nevertheless, regardless of a space project's size, the existing international legal and regulatory framework underpins and permits space activities. This regime is decades old, and was created in a different geopolitical context. Some feel it is ill-suited for the next half-century of space activities—either too restrictive, or not sufficiently clear in its requirements.

Undoubtedly, the legal order will change in the coming years and decades, and hopefully in ways that permit space activities to grow and advance. For the time being, an understanding of the existing international framework—consisting of general international law, treaties specifically applicable to space activities, and various resolutions from the United Nations and from working groups such as the International Organization for Standardization is essential to understanding how any space project can proceed. All new actors in space, whether they are sovereign states expanding their space capabilities, new private ventures with commercial interests in space, or academic and research projects, should be aware of the international framework as examined in this chapter.

ONE | THE INTERNATIONAL FRAMEWORK FOR SPACE ACTIVITIES

The focus of Chapter One is the international legal and regulatory framework, beginning with the rights and obligations of the Outer Space Treaty (OST) and the subsequent space treaties which expand and elaborate upon it, and especially the treaty's obligations in terms of international state responsibility and international registration of space objects. International frequency management is then discussed, as well as remote sensing, broadcasting standards, and international export control measures. Discussion of state liability and the various dispute settlement avenues follows.

Various international environmental concerns are then explored, including protection of the Earth environment, back-contamination of the Earth from space missions, nuclear power sources in space, space debris, and the protection of celestial bodies. To conclude the chapter, more advanced issues are explored, including the unresolved issues related to the lack of a legal definition of where outer space begins, the legal status and protections of humans in space, and the use of space resources.

This international framework for the conduct of space activities should be explored and understood by new state actors seeking to begin or expand their space competencies and by new non-state actors as a general due-diligence to better understand the licensing and regulatory process.

FREEDOM AND RESPONSIBILITY

Three core principles lie at the heart of the international framework for space activities: freedom of exploration and use of space, peaceful purposes, and state responsibility. These principles, as contained in the five core treaties form the foundation of international space law, and are reflected in many of the other legal and political mechanisms that make up the international framework for space activities. The following sections provide an overview of each principle.

Freedom of Exploration and Use of Space

Outer space is free to be explored, and no nation or state can restrict another state's legitimate access to space for peaceful purposes. This freedom is enshrined in the most important source of space law, the Treaty on Principles Governing the Activities of States in the Exploration and Use of Outer Space, including the Moon and Other Celestial Bodies, more commonly referred to as the Outer Space Treaty.

Figure 1 – Signing of the Outer Space Treaty. Soviet Ambassador Anatoly F. Dobrynin, UK Ambassador Sir Patrick Dean, US Ambassador Arthur J. Goldberg, US President Lyndon B. Johnson and others observe as US Secretary of State Dean Rusk signs the Outer Space Treaty on January 27, 1967 in Washington, DC
Source: UNOOSA.

Like all treaties, the Outer Space Treaty balances rights with obligations. The freedoms to use and explore space are balanced with the obligations listed throughout the treaty. Those obligations can be considered positive obligations requiring a state to perform certain actions, or negative obligations that prohibit actions. Article I of the Outer Space Treaty lists these all-important freedoms, explaining that:

> *Outer space, including the Moon and other celestial bodies, shall be free for exploration and use by all States without discrimination of any kind, on a basis of equality and in accordance with international law, and there shall be free access to all areas of celestial bodies.*

This free access means that emerging actors in space have just as much right to explore and use space for peaceful purposes as the established space actors. The preceding clause of Article I also directly states that the activity of exploring and using outer space is the "province of all mankind."

The Outer Space Treaty then requires that "[t]here shall be freedom of scientific investigation in outer space, including the Moon and other celestial bodies, and States shall facilitate and encourage international cooperation in such investigation." Indeed, the very nature of the Outer Space Treaty encourages international cooperation and scientific investigations as ways to promote peace and stability among the nations of the world.

Like most international treaties, the preamble to the Outer Space Treaty does not contain legally operative language establishing rights, obligations, or prohibitions. Rather, it contains the object and purpose of the treaty—the subject matter being addressed, the reason the treaty is being drafted, and what the treaty is intended to establish. The preamble to the Outer Space Treaty explains the motives and aspirations behind the creation of the treaty, formalizing the reasons that states decided to create it; these being because they:

- recognize the common interest of all humankind in the progress of the exploration and use of outer space for peaceful purposes;
- believe that the exploration and use of outer space should be carried out for the benefit of all peoples, irrespective of their degree of economic or scientific development;
- desire to contribute to broad international development of both the scientific and legal aspects of space exploration and use; and
- believe that this international cooperation will drive mutual understanding and strengthen friendly relations among states and peoples.

These beliefs in the preamble to the Outer Space Treaty reflect the intentions of the drafters for creating this new international legal instrument. All international space law should be read with the understanding that these are the intentions and aspirations behind the Outer Space Treaty. No interpretation of space law (whether that law is international or national) should circumvent, subvert, or defeat the motives and purposes listed above. In fact, any valid interpretation of any of the articles of the Outer Space Treaty must reflect, conform, and serve these purposes. These aspirations, contained in the preamble but forming an integral part of the treaty, should always be remembered when considering the freedom to access space, explore space, or partake in any other activity or use of space.

Additionally, it should be noted that the words "exploration" and "use" are in the very title of the Outer Space Treaty. The use of outer space, including the use of the moon and the use of any celestial bodies, was contemplated by the drafters and negotiators of the treaty, and is part of the freedom of access, exploration, and use as codified in Article I. It is important to remember that the freedom to explore outer space is held by all states, and through them, by all peoples of the world. No state can lawfully prevent or restrict any new entrant to the field of peaceful space activities.

While many treaties may address space activities in a tangential fashion, there are five core treaties, listed in Table 1, that address space activities specifically.

The Core Treaties on Space			
Treaty	Adoption by General Assembly	Entered into Force	Number of Ratifying States as of April 2017
Treaty on Principles Governing the Activities of States in the Exploration and Use of Outer Space, including the moon and Other Celestial Bodies *(Outer Space Treaty)*	1966	1967	105
Agreement on the Rescue of Astronauts, the Return of Astronauts and the Return of Objects Launched into Outer Space *(Astronaut Agreement)*	1967	1968	95
Convention on International Liability for Damage Caused by Space Objects *(Liability Convention)*	1971	1972	94
Convention on Registration of Objects Launched into Outer Space (Registration Convention)	1974	1976	63
Agreement Governing the Activities of States on the Moon and Other Celestial Bodies (Moon Agreement)	1979	1984	17

Table 1 – The Core Treaties on Space

The Core Treaties

The core space treaties were negotiated and drafted by the United Nations (UN) Committee on the Peaceful Uses of Outer Space (COPUOS), a standing body of member states of the United Nations that has considered the political, legal, and scientific aspects of space activities since the beginning of the space age. The titles of the treaties in Table 1 illustrate their basic subject matter, and they largely elaborate upon and refine provisions of the foundational Outer Space Treaty. The 1968 Astronaut Rescue and Return Agreement refines and expands on the protection given to astronauts, while the 1972 Liability Convention similarly expands the provisions for liability for damage incurred in the launching and operation of space objects. The Liability Convention establishes absolute liability for physical damage suffered on the surface of the Earth, or to aircraft in flight, and establishes a fault-based liability regime for space objects in outer space. The 1975 Registration Convention makes mandatory both international registration and the establishment of national registries of space objects.

Figure 2 shows the growth in the number of states that are party to the core treaties, along with the relative success of these treaties in relation to one another. As they were all drafted from the mid-1960s until the late 1970s, this era of broad treaty-making by the United Nations is now over, and subsequent decades have seen the United Nations use General Assembly resolutions to communicate principles on a number of subsequent space-related topics.

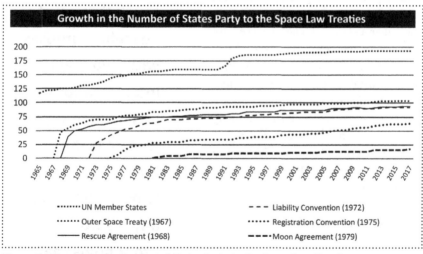

Figure 2 – Growth in the Number of States Party to the Space Law Treaties
Source: Secure World Foundation.

Article III of the Outer Space Treaty incorporates space law into the larger body of international law. Consequently, other sources of public international law, including the UN Charter, impact the law of outer space. The practices of states, along with general principles of law, are also valid and often applicable. For example, one principle of general international law can be summarized as "that which is not explicitly prohibited is otherwise permitted." The consequence of these explicit freedoms, and their context in the larger body of international law, is the creation of a wide scope of state freedom in outer space with only certain particular and explicitly codified legal prohibitions.

For states looking to begin their first forays into space, signing and ratifying the core treaties sends a signal to the world that the rights and obligations of international space law are understood and accepted, and underlies their serious approach to beginning space activities. It shows that they intend to be a responsible and law-abiding actor in space, and that they have "joined the club" of spacefaring nations.

Peaceful Purposes

Article IV of the Outer Space Treaty requires that states refrain from placing nuclear weapons or other weapons of mass destruction into Earth orbit or installing or stationing them on celestial bodies. It further requires that the moon and other celestial bodies be used for exclusively peaceful purposes. Next, it forbids the establishment of military bases, installations, or fortifications on celestial bodies, and also forbids testing weapons and conducting military maneuvers on celestial bodies. A previous international treaty, the Nuclear Test Ban Treaty of 1963, also prohibits states from testing nuclear weapons or performing nuclear explosions beyond the limits of the atmosphere, including in outer space.

There have always been military and security aspects to space activities. As a foundational security treaty negotiated between Cold War powers, the Outer Space Treaty addresses this dual-

There has always been a debate about the definition of peaceful purposes, with two main interpretations arising: one says that peaceful purposes means "non-military" in any regard; the other holds that peaceful merely means "non-aggressive."

use nature of space capabilities. Since the treaty entered into force, there has always been a debate about the definition of peaceful purposes, with two main interpretations arising: one says that peaceful purposes means "non-military" in any regard; the other holds that peaceful merely means "non-aggressive." The latter interpretation has gradually gained broader acceptance. However, the clear prohibitions mentioned above remain.

As other sources of international law are also applicable to space activities through their inclusion in Article III of the Outer Space Treaty, the general prohibition on the threat of, or use of, force between UN Member States is therefore applicable to outer space. Article 2.4 of the UN Charter requires that:

> *[a]ll Members shall refrain in their international relations from the threat or use of force against the territorial integrity or political independence of any state, or in any other manner inconsistent with the Purposes of the United Nations.*

Additionally, Articles 39 to 51 address threats and breaches of the peace, acts of aggression, and the inherent right of self-defense. This general regime of public international law between states underpins the special regime of space law, and creates the same prohibitions and restrictions for military conflict in space as on Earth. However, there is a lack of consensus on the specific applications of international law to conflict in space as exists in the maritime, air, and land domains.

International State Responsibility

In the usual affairs of humankind, governments are not generally responsible for the actions of their citizens. If a citizen of Country A goes abroad to Country B, and someone in Country B wants to bring a claim against them, they don't often also name Country A's government as a defendant. In the usual dealings between people and foreign governments, people are not the responsibility of their governments. This is not the case in outer space activities. In fact, in activities dealing with outer space, the situation is reversed.

Under Article VI of the Outer Space Treaty, states are directly responsible for all their national space activities, whether that activity is conducted by the government itself or by any of its citizens or companies, and whether launching domestically or possibly even when its nationals are conducting space activities abroad. The direct responsibility of national governments is relatively unique in international law. Article VI of the Outer Space Treaty reads:

States Parties to the Treaty shall bear international responsibility for national activities in outer space, including the Moon and other celestial bodies, whether such activities are carried on by governmental agencies or by non-governmental entities, and for assuring that national activities are carried out in conformity with the provisions set forth in the present Treaty.

The second sentence continues:

The activities of non-governmental entities in outer space, including the Moon and other celestial bodies, shall require authorization and continuing supervision by the appropriate State Party to the Treaty.

Because the direct responsibility and potential international liability for all national activities is relatively unique and quite broad, this duty should always be taken into account when considering space activities. The requirement that activities be carried out in conformity with the treaty act as a limiting provision to Article I's freedoms of access, exploration, and use. When space activities cause physical damage on the ground, to aircraft in flight, or to space objects in space, then mere international responsibility expands to international liability, a separate but related issue expanded upon in Chapter One: International Liability.

Today, many space activities are international in nature, and in any multinational space project, all states are under these obligations. This expansive international state responsibility is the incentive for national space policy and space legislation, the subject of Chapter Two.

REGISTRATION OF SPACE OBJECTS

Along with international responsibility for national activities, and potential international liability for damage caused to other states, registration is an obligation placed upon states for their space activities. The tracking of which states are responsible for which activities is aided by registration in both international and national registries of space objects.

International registration of space objects was first called for in United Nations General Assembly (UNGA) Resolution 1721 B (XVI), adopted by the UN at the dawn of the space age in 1961. This resolution calls upon states launching space objects to promptly provide the UN with launch information for a UN-maintained public registry. This international registry was intended to aid other states in determining which activities in space are being conducted by whom. While the original intention of this resolution was to help prevent collisions in space, today this voluntary notification to the UN would be called a transparency and confidence-building measure (TCBM), as notifying the rest of the world about launches also helps show that a state is open about its activities.

While UNGA Res. 1721 B (XVI) is not legally binding and imposes no mandatory obligations on states, international registration of launched space objects was made mandatory in 1975 with the Registration Convention – at least as regards to those states which are a party to that convention. As of 2017, 63 states are party to the Registration Convention, including all the major and historical space powers (albeit quite a few less than the number of states that are party to the Outer Space Treaty).

Articles III and IV of the Registration Convention require that the UN Secretary-General establish a registry of space objects with open access to all. Article IV requires that any launching state placing its launched space object on a national registry shall also communicate to the Secretary-General certain information for the international registry. That information is:

- The name of the launching state (or states)
- An appropriate designator of the space object or its registration number
- Date and territory or location of launch
- Basic orbital parameters, including:
  - Nodal period
  - Inclination
  - Apogee
  - Perigee
- General function of the space object

The remaining requirements include updating the UN with additional information, along with including information on objects that are no longer in Earth orbit. On behalf of the Secretary-General, the United Nations Office for Outer Space Affairs (OOSA) is the keeper of this international registry established by the Registration Convention, as well as the registry of objects registered pursuant to UNGA Res. 1721 B (XVI). For states not party to the Registration Convention, international registration can be made pursuant to UNGA Res. 1721 B (XVI).

OOSA maintains a standard form for both registries which it recommends that states use (see Figure 3). The required registration information is not overly detailed.

UNGA Resolution 62/101

The registry form (Figure 3) also references UNGA Res. 62/101 from 2007 entitled "Recommendations on enhancing the practice of States and international intergovernmental organizations in registering space objects." The resolution expresses a desire for states to proffer additional information regarding space objects, including updated circumstances such as a change of function, non-functional status, change of orbital position, or removal to a disposal orbit, along with the change in status of their owner, operator, or of the space object itself. This ability to update information to the UN is a key advancement and has implications for more advanced or complex space activities such as launches with multiple launching states, and for satellite servicing or debris removal in the future.

National Registration

Article VIII of the Outer Space Treaty does not address international registration. Rather, it discusses national registration, stating that a

> State Party to the Treaty on whose registry an object launched into outer space is carried shall retain jurisdiction and control over such object, and over any personnel thereof, while in outer space or on a celestial body. Ownership of objects launched into outer space, including objects landed or constructed on a celestial body, and of their component parts, is not affected by their presence in outer space or on a celestial body or by their return to the Earth.

In an area where state sovereignty is absent, the effect of this article is to provide a crucial component of state sovereignty, namely jurisdiction. The right of a state to exercise jurisdiction over space objects depends upon that state listing its launched objects on a national registry. Each state might need to consolidate that international right in its national legislation.

Enshrining in an international treaty the national right to exercise jurisdictional powers in an extraterritorial manner through a national registry gives states an incentive to establish national registers, and to list their space objects on them. In so doing, it furthers the transparency of space activities, and as long as national registries are publicly searchable, outsiders can determine which

Part A:
Information provided in conformity with the Registration Convention or
General Assembly Resolution 1721 B (XVI)

New registration of space object	*Yes* ☐	*Check Box*
Additional information for previously registered space object	*Submitted under the Convention: ST/SG/SER.E/* ☐ *Submitted under resolution 1721B: A/AC.105/INF.* ☐	*UN document number in which previous registration data was distributed to Member States*

Launching State/States/international intergovernmental organization

State of registry or international intergovernmental organization		*Under the Registration Convention, only one State of registry can exist for a space object.*
Other launching States		

Designator

Name	
COSPAR international designator	
National designator/registration number as used by State of registry	

Date and territory or location of launch

Date of launch (hours, minutes, seconds optional)	*dd/mm/yyyy*	*hrs*	*min* *sec*	*Coordinated Universal Time (UTC)*
Territory or location of launch				

Basic orbital parameters

Nodal period		*minutes*
Inclination		*degrees*
Apogee		*kilometres*
Perigee		*kilometres*

Figure 3 – OOSA International Registry Form
   Source: UNOOSA.

Part A:
Information provided in conformity with the Registration Convention or General Assembly Resolution 1721 B (XVI)

General function

General function of space object

Change of status

Date of decay/reentry/deorbit (hours, minutes, seconds optional)	dd/mm/yyyy	hrs	min	sec	Coordinated Universal Time (UTC)

Sources of information

UN registration documents	http://www.unoosa.org/oosa/SORegister/docsstatidx.html
COSPAR international designators	http://nssdc.gsfc.nasa.gov/spacewarn/
Global launch locations	http://www.unoosa.org/oosa/SORegister/resources.html
Online Index of Objects Launched into Outer Space	http://www.unoosa.org/oosa/osoindex.html

Part B:
Additional information for use in the United Nations Register of Objects Launched into Outer Space, as recommended in General Assembly Resolution 62/101

Change of status in operations

Date when space object is no longer functional (hours, minutes, seconds optional)	dd/mm/yyyy	hrs	min	sec	Coordinated Universal Time (UTC)
Date when space object is moved to a disposal orbit (hours, minutes, seconds optional)	dd/mm/yyyy	hrs	min	sec	Coordinated Universal Time (UTC)
Physical conditions when space object is moved to a disposal orbit (see COPUOS Space Debris Mitigation Guidelines)					

Basic orbital parameters

Geostationary position (where applicable, planned/actual)		degrees East

Additional Information

Website:

Part C:
Information relating to the change of supervision of a space object, as recommended in General Assembly Resolution 62/101

Change of supervision of the space object

Date of change in supervision *(hours, minutes, seconds optional)*	dd/mm/yyyy	hrs min sec Coordinated Universal Time (UTC)
Identity of the new owner or operator		

Change of orbital position

Previous orbital position		degrees East
New orbital position		degrees East
Change of function of the space object		

Part D:
Additional voluntary information for use in the United Nations Register of Objects Launched into Outer Space

Basic information

Space object owner or operator		
Launch vehicle		
Celestial body space object is orbiting (if not Earth, please specify)		
Other information (information that the State of registry may wish to furnish to the United Nations)		

Sources of information

General Assembly resolution 62/101	http://www.unoosa.org/oosa/SORegister/resources.html
COPUOS Space Debris Mitigation Guidelines	http://www.unoosa.org/oosa/SORegister/resources.html
Texts of the Registration Convention and relevant resolutions	http://www.unoosa.org/oosa/SORegister/resources.html

space objects belong to which country. Coupled with this are the final sections of Article VIII, whereby states retain ownership of their launched space objects and their component parts while in outer space and upon return to Earth. States becoming party to the Outer Space Treaty and subsequent treaties should consider establishing and maintaining national space registries.

Currently, over 30 states have national space registries, and some make their national registries available and searchable online (although this is not a requirement). While international organizations cannot be parties to the Registration Convention, the European Space Agency (ESA) and the European Organisation for the Exploitation of Meteorological Satellites (EUMETSAT) also keep registries of their space objects. As the method for exercising jurisdiction over launched space objects, the national registry is an important component of a state's oversight and responsibility requirements. National registration is discussed further in Chapter Two: National Registration.

Suborbital Launches

The Registration Convention requires registration of objects "launched into Earth orbit or beyond," and the previous UNGA resolution likewise calls for registration of objects "launched into orbit or beyond." However, there is no international requirement or call to register objects that are only being launched for suborbital operations. How to deal with suborbital space activities is an open question that new actors will need to consider from a registration perspective, as registration may impact whether suborbital activities are considered to be "space activities."

To the extent that a state's suborbital activities take place solely above their national airspace and no other international aspects or elements are involved, these suborbital activities seem to be purely the national space activities of a single state. Launches that

> How to deal with suborbital space activities is an open question that new actors will need to consider from a registration perspective, as registration may impact whether suborbital activities are considered to be "space activities."

go higher in altitude than some orbits, but have insufficient speed or are placed on a parabolic trajectory and return to Earth, are therefore also not considered "orbital." To date, many states haven't made a legal determination whether and to what extent international space law is applicable to suborbital activities.

However, one of the main goals of international registration is to alert the world to a state's space activities. Consequently, continuing to observe the above-mentioned international registration requirements fulfills these objectives of international transparency and confidence-building about national space activities.

INTERNATIONAL FREQUENCY MANAGEMENT

Spacecraft communicate using frequencies in the electromagnetic spectrum that are limited by physics. Consequently, frequency coordination and allocation among users is one of the most important processes for the successful operation of a space project.

The International Telecommunication Union (ITU) is a specialized agency of the United Nations. The oldest organization within the UN system, the ITU traces its origin to international postal unions in the mid-19th century. Today, the ITU has over 190 member states that are party to its principal treaties: the ITU Constitution and the ITU Convention. Since the beginning of the space age, the ITU has aided the exploration and use of space through international coordination and frequency allocation. The ITU is tasked with ensuring the rational, equitable, efficient, and economical use of the radiofrequency spectrum. Within the ITU, this task is primarily managed by the ITU Radiocommunication (ITU-R) sector.It also administers orbital positions (called "slots") in geostationary Earth orbit (GEO). GEO is a limited natural resource in the sense that its use for satellite applications requires coordination between users to prevent congestion and misuse.

The ITU-R maintains the ITU Radio Regulations, which include the administrative regulations for radio communication services including satellite radio communication services. The Radio Regulations include the Master International Frequency Register (MIFR) of all coordinated frequencies. The Master International Frequency Register should be consulted very early in a space project, when considering which frequency or frequencies a space project's space systems and Earth stations will use.

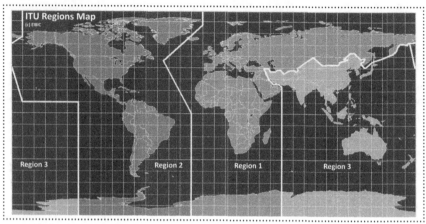

Figure 4 – ITU World Regions
Source: ITU.

The ITU divides the world into three administrative regions, as shown in Figure 4. Region One includes Europe, Africa, the former countries of the Soviet Union, and Mongolia. Region Two includes the Americas and Greenland. Region Three is the rest of Asia, Australasia, and the Pacific. Each administrative region has assigned particular frequencies to particular technologies and services. The ITU has allocated a number of frequencies for specific space activities, including frequencies for Earth exploration, meteorology, radio astronomy, emergency telecommunications, radio navigation, space operations, space research, and amateur satellites.

Radiofrequency spectrum is divided into bands that are either exclusively allocated or that share allocations for various applications. Applications with broad international usage enjoy exclusive allocations. A shared portion of the spectrum is available for one or more services, either on a worldwide or regional basis. Within the shared bands, different services are classed into either primary or secondary services. Primary services enjoy superior rights to secondary services.

The Radio Regulations require that secondary services:

- not cause harmful interference to stations of primary services to which frequencies are already assigned or may be assigned at a later date;
- cannot claim protection from harmful interference from stations or a primary service to which frequencies are already assigned or may be assigned at a later date; and
- can, however, claim protection from harmful interference from stations of the same or other secondary services to which frequencies may be assigned at a later date.

Figure 5 shows the distribution of applications into different parts of the spectrum, each of which also depends on the region of the world in which that use is located.

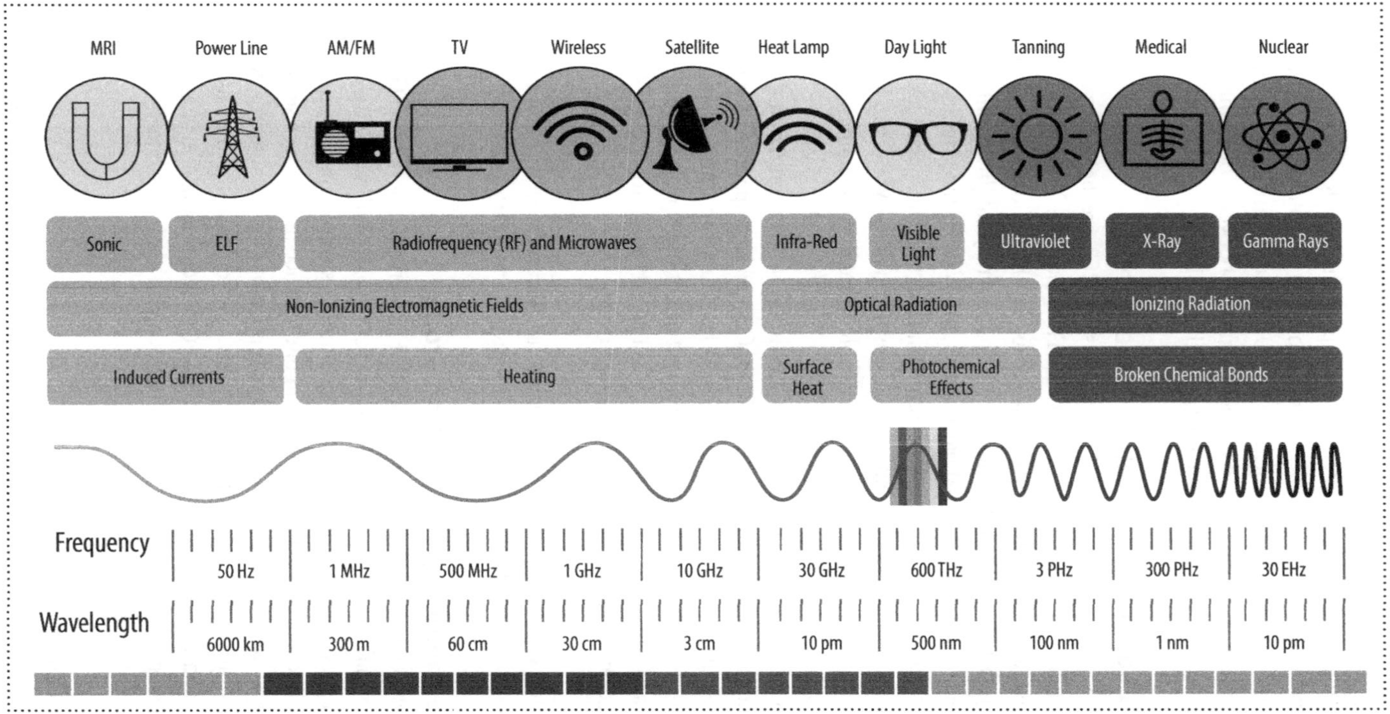

Figure 5 – The Electromagnetic Spectrum, Including Uses Along the Spectrum

Source: Secure World Foundation.

National administrators implement and apply the ITU Radio Regulations on the national level. A deeper discussion follows in Chapter Two, dealing with the procedure of coordinating with the ITU through national administrators, and in Chapter Three, dealing with coordination between operators and national administrators, and among the operators themselves.

World Radiocommunication Conference

World Radiocommunication Conferences (WRC) are held every three to four years, under the auspices of the ITU-R. Their purpose is to allow member states to review and revise the treaty deciding use of the radio-frequency spectrum and of the geostationary satellite and non-geostationary satellite orbit. A month-long conference with thousands of participants, the WRC is the primary venue through which frequency assignments for terrestrial, aerial, and space-based applications are reviewed and made. As such, decisions taken at the WRC can have significant impact on the spectrum resources available to satellite operators.

The WRC also determines the "Questions" for examination by the Radio-communications Assembly and its Study Groups in preparation for future WRCs. Because agendas and questions are set so far in advance, new space actors should determine what areas being studied might affect their project plans and spectrum needs and whether they themselves need to advocate for changes to the Radio Regulations to accommodate their future plans.

Companies and other interested parties can become sector members of the ITU, allowing them to observe meetings and provide industry perspective.

Space Frequency Coordination Group

An additional notable group is the Space Frequency Coordination Group (SFCG), an informal group of frequency managers from civil space agencies. Annual meetings of the group are held to create administrative and technical agreements about allocated bands in order to avoid interference in the space sector. The SFCG meetings adopts resolutions and recommendations containing technical and administrative agreements for space agencies to make the best use of allocated bands, and to avoid interference. The SFCG recommendations are not formally binding, and their effectiveness depends upon their voluntary acceptance and implementation by member agencies.

Laser Communications

In recent years, there has been considerable advancement in the development of laser communications systems for satellites. Unlike radio communications, which utilize signals in the radio part of the electromagnetic spectrum, laser communications utilize signals in the optical part of the electromagnetic spectrum. Laser technologies have been demonstrated for communicating between ground stations and satellites orbiting the Earth, between two satellites orbiting the Earth, and between satellites orbiting the moon and Mars and ground stations on Earth.

There are several major differences between traditional radio satellite communications and laser communications. Laser communications are line-of-sight, meaning that there must be a clear, direct line path between the transmitter and receiver. This means that laser communications are not able to broadcast over a wide reception footprint. But this also makes laser communications much harder to intercept, and there is very little chance of unintentional interference. Laser communications also use much higher frequencies than radio communications, which means they are able to carry much more data.

Laser communications pose significant questions for international regulation. Under the current definitions adopted by the ITU, satellites utilizing laser communications do not currently require a license. The ITU Radio Regulations Board is currently restricted to regulating the radiofrequency spectrum used for broadcast applications, which does not apply to laser communications. However, there are some who feel the definition of satellite communication should be expanded to cover laser communications, as the assignment of spectrum licenses is currently one of the few ways to regulate space activities.

REMOTE SENSING

Each state enjoys sovereignty over its territory, and therefore states are often concerned about others gaining insight into what is happening within their territory, either for commercial, political, or military purposes. So while space is free to be explored, many states feel some uneasiness about spacecraft turning their cameras back towards Earth, enabling neighbors to gain information.

To date, no international treaty directly governs remote sensing. Rather, a number of UNGA resolutions establish certain principles relevant to remote sensing. UNGA Resolution 41/65 of 1986 relates fifteen principles for states to follow in their remote sensing activities. The resolution first establishes a difference between "primary data" and "processed data." Primary data means those "raw data that are acquired by remote sensors borne by a space object and that are transmitted or delivered to the ground from space." Conversely, processed data means the "products resulting from the processing of the primary data." Analyzed information is defined as "information resulting from the interpretation of processed data, inputs of data, and knowledge from other sources."

Principle XII of UNGA 41/65 is perhaps the most important of the remote sensing principles, and strikes a balance between the freedom to explore space and the concerns states have about being observed ("sensed states"):

> As soon as the primary data and the processed data concerning the territory under its jurisdiction is produced, the sensed State shall have access to them on a non-discriminatory basis and on reasonable cost terms. The sensed State shall also have access to the available analysed information concerning the territory under its jurisdiction in the possession of any State participating in remote sensing activities on the same basis and terms, taking particularly into account the needs and interests of the developing countries.

While Resolution 41/65 is a non-binding resolution from the United Nations General Assembly, it is meant to reflect the best practices of spacefaring states. Beyond this resolution, data-sharing has become a key principle in remote sensing activities because of an early recognition of the links between accessibility to such data and societal benefits, scientific progress, and commercial applications.

Open data-exchange at the international level has been upheld especially for global meteorological data and related products, as adopted in World Meteorological Organization (WMO) Resolution 40. The Group on Earth Observations (GEO), a partnership of governments and organizations working towards coordinated, comprehensive, and sustained Earth observations and information, actively promotes full and open data-sharing of integrated observations to address challenges at the global, regional, national, and local levels.

INTERNATIONAL STANDARDS

International standards are accepted in many fields in order to increase safety, reliability, and quality, and are increasingly being implemented in the space field. A standard is merely a document that provides requirements, specifications, guidelines, or characteristics that can be used consistently to ensure that materials, products, processes, and services are fit for their purposes. Standards can be as specific as an outline on how to interface with a particular class of device, or as general as providing details around management best practices for ensuring quality.

While standards can be developed by any organization or entity, international standards are becoming increasingly important in a more globalized world. Adopting an international standard can help ensure compatibility across entire global sectors and can also be used by companies to signal to potential customers that their products or services are high-quality. Multiple organizations in a sector can use standards to codify lessons learned from past mistakes to help improve overall safety in a sector.

International Organization for Standardization

The primary international standards body is the International Organization for Standardization (ISO). ISO is an independent, non-governmental organization created in 1946 to facilitate the international coordination and unification of industrial standards. The ISO membership consists of the primary national standards body from more than 160 participating countries. Individuals or companies cannot become members, but can be appointed by their national standards bodies as representatives in the areas of technical standards and policy development.

Although many of the ISO standards apply in some way to the space sector, there is one technical committee, TC20, that is focused on aircraft and space vehicles. Within TC20, the bulk of the space standards are developed by two subcommittees: subcommittee 13 (SC13)–Space Data and Information Transfer Systems, and subcommittee 14 (SC14)–Space Systems and Operations. Each subcommittee has multiple working groups that each focus on a specific area, such as systems engineering, operations and ground support, and orbital debris.

ITU Telecommunication Standardization Sector

The Telecommunication Standardization Sector (ITU-T) is the division of the ITU responsible for coordinating technical standards for telecommunications. It does this through a consensus-based approach with both member states and sector members providing input to the numerous study groups. The purpose of the study groups is to develop "Recommendations" and other technical documents, which become mandatory only when adopted as part of a national law.

The World Telecommunication Standardization Assembly (WTSA), which meets every four years, approves the study groups, sets their work programme for the next four-year period, and appoints their chairmen and vice-chairmen.

Though not as important for space actors as the ITU-R, the ITU-T has study groups looking at cybersecurity, the Internet of Things (IOT), 5G, and other topics of interest to some companies.

Consultative Committee for Space Data Systems
The Consultative Committee for Space Data Systems (CCSDS) was founded in 1982 by several major space agencies to provide a forum for discussing common problems in developing and operating space data systems. There are currently 11 space agencies that are full members of CCSDS and 28 observer agencies. The main focus of CCSDS is developing standards for common space-data-handling needs, and specifically transferring data from satellites to terrestrial receivers. The CCSDS has developed standards for the following areas:

- Spacecraft Onboard Interface Services
- Space Link Services
- Space Internetworking Services
- Mission Operations and Information Management Services
- Systems Engineering
- Cross-Support Services

Although officially separate organizations, ISO and CCSDS have developed close links for space standards. Standards adopted by CCSDS are also ISO standards under subcommittee 13.

International Committee on Global Navigation Satellite Systems
The proliferation of space technologies has led to the emergence of proposed international standards in other areas such as global navigation satellite systems (GNSS) and geospatial information. The International Committee on Global Navigation Satellite Systems (ICG), established in 2005, promotes voluntary cooperation on civil satellite-based positioning, navigation, timing, and value-added services. Through its Providers Forum—which includes China, India, Japan, the European Union (EU), the Russian Federation, and the US—the ICG encourages coordination among current and future GNSS providers to ensure greater compatibility, interoperability, and transparency.

United Nations Committee of Experts on Global Geospatial Information Management

In the field of geospatial information, the United Nations Committee of Experts on Global Geospatial Information Management (UN-GGIM), established in 2011, provides a forum for coordination and exchange among member states and international organizations while promoting the development of global geospatial information and its use in addressing global challenges. Key UN-GGIM initiatives integrate efforts to promote technical standards to advance interoperability priority datasets while promoting engagement on legal and policy issues and related issues impacting national and regional capacity for geospatial information. Complementary to the work of the UN-GGIM, the Open Geospatial Consortium (OGC), an international industry consortium of companies, government agencies, and universities, drives the development of publicly available interface standards to support the interoperability and accessibility of geospatial information and services.

INTERNATIONAL EXPORT CONTROL

There is significant international concern over the uncontrolled spread of both conventional military goods and technologies and dual-use technology such as space technology. Dual-use technology is commonly defined as technology having both civil and military applications. An example in the space industry is the chemical rocket, which can be used as a space launch vehicle to place satellites and humans into orbit, but which can also serve as a ballistic missile for delivering weapons of mass destruction. All new actors, including private non-governmental space actors, should be acutely aware of the sensitive nature and politically charged context of all space activities.

At the international level, the Wassenaar Arrangement on Export Controls for Conventional Arms and Dual-Use Goods and Technologies is a significant effort to control the proliferation of specific types of military and dual-use goods and technologies. It was established in 1996 and currently has 41 participating states, mostly located in North America and Europe. The goal of the Wassenaar Arrangement is to contribute to regional and international security and stability by promoting transparency and greater responsibility for transfers of conventional arms and dual-use goods and technologies, thus preventing destabilizing accumulations. Participating states control items in the "List of Dual-Use Goods and Technologies and Munitions List" and work to prevent unauthorized transfers of those items. The arrangement also uses export controls as a way to combat terrorism, and is not designed to work against any particular state or group of states. Participating states agree to exchange information on sensitive dual-use goods and technologies, follow agreed-upon best practices, and report any transfers or denied transfers of controlled items made to recipients outside of the Arrangement.

The Missile Technology Control Regime (MTCR) is another important international control in the realm of space activities. The MTCR is a voluntary regime that was originally established in 1987, and in 2017 has 34 participating countries. Four additional countries have agreed to abide by MTCR export control rules but have not formally joined. The goal of the MTCR is to coordinate national export licensing efforts in order to prevent the proliferation of uninhabited delivery systems capable of delivering weapons of mass destruction.

In 2002, the Hague International Code of Conduct against Ballistic Missile Proliferation, also known as the Hague Code of Conduct, was created to augment the MTCR. The Hague Code of Conduct calls on participating states to exercise restraint in the testing, production, and export of ballistic missiles. While the Hague Code is less restrictive than the MTCR, with 119 participating states it has significantly more international acceptance, and it serves as a solid TCBM. Subscribing states agree to making pre-launch notifications and annual declarations of their policies.

One country's export control laws have had global effects. The United States' International Traffic in Arms Regulations (ITAR), a set of government regulations that control the export and import of defense-related articles and services on the US Munitions List (USML), have affected how other countries develop domestic industries because of rules requiring "ITAR compliance." Part of this depends upon registering with the US State Department's Directorate of Defense Trade Controls (DDTC) and obtaining relevant licenses when necessary. Items on the USML include some satellites and their related technologies. Alternatively, some states have successfully marketed their products as being "ITAR-free," meaning that they would not have as many of the exporting restrictions that items on the USML would have.

INTERNATIONAL LIABILITY

In international law, liability is a concept related to but altogether distinct from responsibility. Article VII of the Outer Space Treaty establishes the obligation that states launching space objects shall be internationally liable for

damage to another State Party to the Treaty or to its natural or juridical persons by such object or its component parts on the Earth, in air space or in outer space, including the Moon or other celestial bodies.

This obligation to be held liable for resulting damage is necessarily linked with responsibility, but is distinct enough to require close attention. Whereas responsibility, discussed above, is an obligation to ensure that all national activities are carried out in conformity with the Outer Space Treaty, the liability provision requires that states undertake action towards the compensation of other states should certain damages occur. The definition of damage, as contained in the 1972 Liability Convention, is "loss of life, personal injury or other impairment of health; or loss of or damage to property or of persons, natural or juridical, or property of international intergovernmental organizations," and is usually interpreted to mean actual physical damage rather than pecuniary interests or other forms of non-physical damage.

Additionally, responsibility is placed on the state or states responsible for national activities. Liability may be imposed upon any "launching state" of space objects causing damage. While space launches are inherently dangerous, and the execution of a launch is not illegal per se, the imposition of liability for damages means that states shall offer compensation after damage occurs, with an understanding that no violation of international law is necessarily found if damage occurs.

The Outer Space Treaty defines four categories of launching state: (1) the state "that launches," (2) that which "procures the launching of a space object," and each state from whose (3) territory or (4) facility an object is launched. The Liability Convention and the Registration Convention reiterate these categories. Consequently, there may be more than one launching state for the purposes of liability. Indeed, this is how many space activities are conducted today.

For states, the liability obligation means that while they are at liberty to conduct launches, they must ensure that they are otherwise lawful, and they must be ready to pay compensation to other states should certain damages occur (either on the ground, in the air, or in space). While a launch may take place from another country's territory, a state may still be exposed to potential liability if its activities fall within one of the four broad categories of launching state. In multilateral space activities, it makes sense for state partners to determine beforehand who will be considered a launching state.

In short, states are both responsible for all their national space activities and potentially liable for activities in which they are considered the launching state. For new entrants to the field of space activities, these obligations mean that supervising states should seek to limit risky launches or those that might cause damage to other states. The supervising state may also put in place provisions to reduce or offset their potential exposure to liability, such as requiring that new non-governmental entrants find insurance for their missions should damage occur. Insurance is discussed in both Chapters Two and Three.

Because a launching state will be held accountable for any resulting damage, any state that is a launching state will be interested in regulating private activities. Once a state is a "launching state," it will always be considered a launching state, and while there can be more than one launching state, there should usually be only one state which is the registering state. It might seem that a launching state would always be a registering state, but complex international launches happen more and more frequently. While being deemed a launching state is tied to the concept of liability, registering is tied more to responsibility for oversight, licensing, and supervision, as well as jurisdictional competency over the space object.

States seeking to foster domestic space activities and industries should consider what regulatory frameworks they should adopt to authorize and supervise these activities.

States seeking to foster domestic space activities and industries should consider what regulatory frameworks they should adopt to authorize and supervise these activities.

DISPUTE SETTLEMENT

Though the desired outcome of any space activity would ideally never include a need for dispute resolution, either among states or private parties or a combination of the two, it is essential to consider which dispute resolution mechanisms are available if needed. This section addresses the basic mechanisms of dispute resolution open to states and private parties.

The 1972 Liability Convention provides a framework by which states can pursue claims for damage caused by a space object—to another space object, to aircraft in flight, or on the surface of Earth. The Liability Convention sets out specific parameters for diplomatic claim resolution, beginning in Article IX. According to Article X of the Liability Convention, "A claim for compensation for damage may be presented to a Launching State no later than one year following the date of the occurrence of the damage or the identification of the Launching State which is liable."

Pursuit of a claim under the Liability Convention does not require the prior exhaustion of remedies in national courts. While a claim can be pursued either in national courts or through the Liability Convention, both avenues cannot be pursued concurrently.

If one or both parties to a dispute are not party to the Liability Convention, the Liability Convention does not apply. In that situation, any diplomatic resolution must follow the rules of international law that otherwise apply to the relevant states that are party to the dispute. For example, if both states are parties to the Outer Space Treaty, the provisions of Article VII of the treaty would apply.

Where a resolution cannot be achieved through diplomatic channels, the Liability Convention provides for the non-adversarial settlement of disputes in the context of a three-member claims commission, which can be initiated by either party to the dispute. The procedure for the formation of a claims commission is described in Articles XIV through XX. Whether they are resolved through diplomatic channels or through a claims commission, disputes decided under the Liability Convention are "determined in accordance with international law and the principles of justice and equity," which generally attempt to restore the state that suffered damage to the position they would have been in had the damage not occurred.

International Court of Justice

With regard to the settlement of space-related disputes between states, the International Court of Justice (ICJ) provides yet another option. Of course, the parties to a dispute must either agree to refer the dispute to the ICJ or recognize compulsory jurisdiction under the ICJ statute. Only states may bring claims to the ICJ (though certain international organizations can pursue advisory opinions). While the ICJ has yet to decide a space-related case to date, it would have subject-matter jurisdiction over any space dispute that would be considered a dispute of international law.

Arbitration and Mediation

Arbitration agreements usually take the form of a clause in a contract setting forth the rights and responsibilities of the parties. Such arbitration clauses are globally well-recognized and are even favored in some jurisdictions, as they reduce the burden on court systems. However, not all parties share the same priorities for dispute resolution. An arbitration clause provides the parties with the authority to establish the arbitrator selection process and set arbitrator qualifications, and to determine whether and what discovery is available, what rules apply (evidentiary and procedural), scheduling, level of confidentiality, the role the arbitrators will serve, decision format and whether the decision is binding, the appeal process if any, choice of law, provisional remedies, and methods of enforcement. Arbitration clauses can specify a particular arbitral tribunal, in which case the parties must comply with the rules and requirements of that tribunal.

Mediation, like both arbitration and adjudication, also employs neutral third parties to resolve a dispute. However, the mediator(s) would not issue a binding decision. The procedures for mediation are less structured and more flexible than those followed by either courts or arbitral tribunals and can be entirely consensual or court-ordered. Resolution of disputes between non-governmental actors, such as corporations or other private entities, is dealt with in the following chapters.

In 2011, the Permanent Court of Arbitration (PCA), situated in The Hague, Netherlands, promulgated its Optional Rules for Arbitration of Disputes Relating to Outer Space Activities. Additionally, the PCA recommends a model clause for insertion into contracts. These rules establish an alternative means of settling disputes among states, international organizations, and private entities.

ENVIRONMENTAL ISSUES

Protection of both terrestrial and space environments is necessary in order to ensure their continued habitability and usability. Space activities, particularly launches, are considered to be inherently dangerous and risky. Consequently, there are various laws and regulations addressing the protection of the environment that forbid certain activities or delineate who is responsible when damage occurs. There are also various principles for protecting the space environment, especially the particularly useful orbits and celestial bodies.

Protection of the Earth Environment
Launching into space is an inherently dangerous activity, usually involving the combustion of large amounts of solid and liquid fuel and the rapid transit of advanced hardware through harsh and unforgiving environments. For that reason, launch sites are chosen in isolated places, far from where accidents can cause harm to others.

A number of sources of law address protecting the Earth environment and allocate the burden of making compensation in case damage happens. On the international level, states are generally responsible for transboundary international harm they cause to other states. This obligation exists in the general custom of states, and is widely recognized. Particular to space law, Article VII of the Outer Space Treaty creates the liability rules for space launches, and includes liability for launching states causing damage on the Earth or in airspace to other states of the treaty.

Additionally, states are absolutely liable for damage their space launches cause on the surface of the ground, or damage to aircraft in flight. This absolute liability does not require that any fault or negligence be proven, merely that the damage occurred resulting from the activities of the responsible state. Consequently, while space activities are generally lawful, their ultra-hazardous nature is reflected in this absolute liability regime from the Outer Space Treaty and the Liability Convention.

Back-Contamination of Earth
Article IX of the Outer Space Treaty largely concerns protecting the space environment, but the second sentence concerns protecting the Earth environment from space material. It reads:

States Parties to the Treaty shall pursue studies in outer space, including the moon and other celestial bodies, and conduct exploration of them so as to avoid their harmful contamination and also adverse changes in the environment of the Earth resulting from the introduction of extraterrestrial matter and, where necessary, shall adopt appropriate measures for this purpose.

The International Committee on Space Research (COSPAR) is an interdisciplinary science organization that has long been concerned with protecting the unique and pristine conditions of space environments—pristine at least in relation to humankind's interaction with them. To this end, COSPAR has promulgated planetary protection principles for space missions, and while the protection of other celestial bodies is discussed below, COSPAR's highest levels of precaution are recommended for Earth-return missions, which may cause so-called "back-contamination."

COSPAR subdivides Earth-return missions into "Restricted Earth Returns" and "Unrestricted Earth Returns." The Unrestricted Earth Return classification applies to missions returning from celestial bodies such as the moon and Venus, which have neither indigenous life forms nor the types of environments where life could flourish. Restricted Earth Return applies to missions returning from Mars and Europa, for example. Future Earth-return missions will be categorized prior to sample return, and others (to be determined by COSPAR when necessary).

Use of Nuclear Power Sources in Space

Powering a spacecraft in the harsh environment of outer space requires recourse to ingenious techniques and technologies. Nuclear power sources have been used on spacecraft since the beginning of the space age. The steady and predictable decay of radioactive material gives off energy in amounts and in a manner suitable for a spacecraft's needs. Radioisotope thermoelectric generators (RTGs) and radioisotope heat units (RHUs) are historically proven methods of power generation, with both the US and the Russian Federation utilizing nuclear power sources.

Recognizing the particular suitability of nuclear power sources for space missions, UNGA Resolution 47/68 of 1992 establishes 11 principles relevant to their use. The nuclear power principles reiterate the applicability of international law and the concepts and framework already established by the Outer Space Treaty and the Liability Convention regarding the responsibility for and potential liability of the launching state, and the jurisdiction and control of the registering state.

Principle 3 of the resolution discusses guidelines and criteria for use, stating that nuclear power sources in space shall be restricted to those missions that "cannot be operated by non-nuclear energy sources in a reasonable manner." It further requires that nuclear reactors shall only use highly enriched uranium–235 as fuel, and that reactors shall be designed and constructed so that they can only become critical upon reaching orbit or interplanetary trajectory, and through no other way (including rocket explosion, re-entry, or impact with water or land.)

Principle 5 contains instructions for making notifications about malfunctioning nuclear power sources that risk re-entry of radioactive materials to Earth. The information to be furnished includes basic launch and orbital parameters as well as information on the nuclear power source itself and the probable physical form, amount, and general radiological characteristics of the components likely to reach the ground. The notification should be sent to concerned states and to the UN Secretary-General. The principles further call for consultations and assistance between states, and reinforce the roles of responsibility, liability and compensation, and the settlement of disputes from the existing space treaties.

Subsequent to UNGA Res. 47/68, the Scientific and Technical Subcommittee of COPUOS worked jointly with the International Atomic Energy Agency to develop the Safety Framework for Nuclear Power Applications in Outer Space. This framework, though not legally binding, is intended to be used as a guide for national and intergovernmental safety purposes. The framework deals with the safe use of nuclear power sources in space mission and contains guidance for governments on how to authorize nuclear power-sourced space missions, guidance for the management of responsibility and safety roles of such missions, and technical guidance. When planned space missions involve nuclear power sources, these guidelines should be consulted early in the project.

Space Debris

After more than 60 years of space activities, humanity has created a significant amount of space debris (Figure 6). Space debris is generally defined as the non-operational satellites, spent rocket stages, and other bits and pieces created during the launch and operation of satellites. The US military currently tracks approximately 23,000 pieces of human-generated debris larger than 10 centimeters (4 inches) in size in Earth orbit, each of which could destroy an active satellite in a collision. Research done by scientists from various space agencies estimates there are 500,000 pieces of space debris between 1 and 10 centimeters (0.4 to 4 inches) in size that are largely untracked, each of which could severely damage an active

Figure 6 – Orbital trajectories for currently tracked satellites and space debris in low Earth orbit. Source: Analytical Graphics Inc.

satellite in a collision. This debris is concentrated in the most heavily used regions of Earth orbit, where many active satellites also reside. These regions include the low Earth orbit (LEO) region below 2,000 kilometers (1,200 miles) in altitude and the geosynchronous region, approximately 36,000 kilometers (22,000 miles) above the equator.

Former US National Aeronautics and Space Administration (NASA) scientist Donald Kessler was one of the first to predict what has since become known as the Kessler Syndrome: as the amount of space debris in orbit grows, a critical point will be reached where the density of space debris will lead to random collisions between space debris. These random collisions would in turn generate more debris at a rate faster than it can be removed from orbit by the Earth's atmosphere. Unlike the dramatic scenario presented in the movie *Gravity*, this process would take place much more slowly over decades or centuries. Space was not a pristine environment before humans began to fill it with satellites, and there has always

The Kessler Syndrome: as the amount of space debris in orbit grows, a critical point will be reached where the density of space debris will lead to random collisions between space debris.

been natural debris in space due to meteoroids. Kessler's prediction was that these cascading debris-on-debris collisions would result in a human-generated debris population that would pose more of a threat to satellites than the natural debris pose.

There is now a general consensus among scientists that this critical point has come to pass, and there is enough human-generated space debris concentrated in the critical region in LEO between 700 and 900 kilometers (430 to 560 miles) to create more debris even if no new satellites were launched. These debris-on-debris collisions will not lead to an infinite growth in the debris population. Rather, they will lead to a future equilibrium point that has a larger population of debris than today. The growth of debris will increase the risks—and thus the associated costs—of operating satellites in critical regions such as LEO. These increased costs could result from the need for more spare satellites to replace those lost in collisions, the need for heavier and more-engineered satellites that cost more to build and launch, and increased operating costs resulting from trying to detect and avoid potential collisions. These rising costs will likely hinder commercial development of space and will place additional pressure on government budgets, potentially resulting in the loss of some of the benefits currently derived from space, or preventing discovery of new benefits.

Efforts to tackle the problem of space debris fall into three major categories: debris mitigation, active debris removal, and space traffic management. Each category addresses a different aspect of the problem: limiting the creation of new space debris, addressing the legacy population of space debris already in orbit, and minimizing the negative impact of the existing debris on space activities.

Debris mitigation includes designing satellites and space systems to minimize the amount of debris they release during normal operations, developing methods to reduce the risk of fragmentation or explosion at end-of-life by venting leftover fuel or discharging batteries, and properly disposing of spacecraft and spent rocket stages after they are no longer useful. In the late 1990s, several major space agencies came together to form the Inter-Agency Space Debris Coordination Committee (IADC). The purpose of the IADC is to help coordinate and share research on space debris among participating space agencies. In 2007, the IADC published the Space Debris Mitigation Guidelines. These technical guidelines define specific protected regions of Earth orbit and the recommended operational practices satellite operators should take to minimize the creation of long-lived space debris in the protected regions. Figure 7 illustrates the various protected regions per the IADC guidelines.

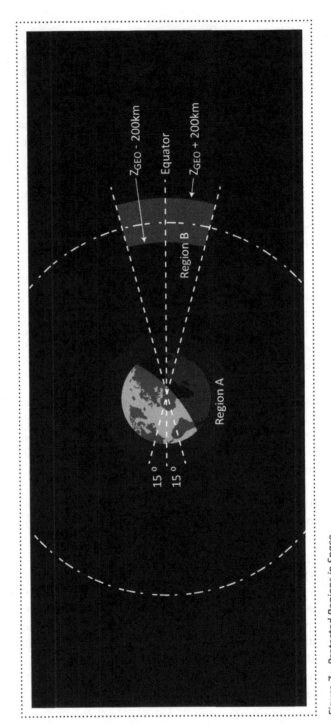

Figure 7 – Protected Regions in Space
Source: Secure World Foundation.

A simplified set of guidelines, the COPUOS space debris mitigation guidelines, which were more political in nature, were endorsed by the United Nations in 2009, although they also remained voluntary. Several states have implemented the debris mitigation guidelines through national regulations and policy, which will be discussed in Chapter Two.

In recent years, the IADC has focused its research efforts on active debris removal (ADR). In 2013, it published a study conducted by six space agencies using six different models which found an average increase of 30 percent in the LEO space debris population over the next 200 years, even with 90 percent adherence to the debris mitigation guidelines. This has provided increased emphasis on the need to start ADR in the near future.

Currently, the discussion on ADR includes three main approaches. The first approach is an effort to remove between five and ten of the most massive space debris objects per year. This would have the effect of slowing or perhaps even halting the long-term growth in the space debris population, but it would not address the near-term collision risk. The second approach is to focus on removing smaller pieces in the 1 to 10 centimeter size range. This would help reduce the short-term risk to satellites, but would have only a minimal impact on the long-term population growth of debris. The third approach is called just-in-time collision avoidance and involves predicting future collisions between two debris objects and altering their orbital trajectories to prevent the collision. Proposed methods for doing so include ground- or space-based lasers or frozen water mist.

Technical experts from around the world have been working intensively on both of these problems over the last several years, and there are some promising technical solutions for removing either large objects or small objects. However, efforts are largely

Solving the challenges of space debris will require close coordination and cooperation among the engineers and scientists working on the technology, as well as the lawyers and policymakers developing policy and regulatory oversight.

a choice between the goals. There is unlikely to be a single, all-encompassing solution that can deal with both large and small debris objectives. Moreover, none of these techniques has been operationally demonstrated in orbit and all of them pose a wide range of legal, policy, and other non-technical challenges.

Solving the challenges of space debris will require close coordination and cooperation among the engineers and scientists working on the technology, as well as the lawyers and policymakers developing policy and regulatory oversight.

ADVANCED ISSUES

The preceding sections discussed important aspects of the international political, legal, and regulatory framework for space activities. Though subtleties exist at the boundaries of each of those topics, much is settled and understood. The last section of this chapter will discuss evolving issues and more advanced topics in space activities.

Boundary Between Airspace and Outer Space

Despite over half a century of space activities, there is no internationally recognized legal definition of where airspace ends and where outer space begins. Neither the Outer Space Treaty nor any other international legal instrument specifies a beginning or bottom point above which outer space begins. A definition of outer space is important because the legal regimes governing airspace and outer space are fundamentally different, and because getting to outer space requires crossing through airspace. A distinction between these two domains would help clarify which legal regime governs activities that cross between them.

Sovereignty, a fundamental component of the modern state, is essentially the power of a government to impose its exclusive authority—by creating laws, by deciding disputes, and through related powers such as enforcing its laws and judicial decisions. A state is exclusively sovereign in the airspace above its territory and territorial waters. However, Article II of the Outer Space Treaty severely undercuts state sovereignty in outer space, leaving only jurisdiction and ownership rights to a state's launched and registered space objects and personnel thereof. In air law, state sovereignty over airspace includes the right to keep others out, and only through complex bilateral and multilateral treaties do states allow civil aircraft from other states to enter (pass through, land on, and take off from) their sovereign airspace. This structure is the opposite of the regime for outer space; all states enjoy the right to freely access, explore, and use outer space.

In 1976, a number of countries in the equatorial regions of the globe signed on to the Bogotá Declaration, asserting a legal claim to control the use of space above their own territory. The declaration sought to upend the existing legal structure by stating that the geostationary orbit, as a finite resource, "must not be considered part of the outer space." While Colombia's Constitution continues to recognize the orbital slot above the country as part of its territory, the Bogotá Declaration's claims have not been widely recognized and states continue to defer to ITU allocations of geostationary slots.

Some feel that this issue—the lack of a legal boundary between airspace and outer space—may increase in relevance in the near future. Some activities might be considered to be occurring in airspace and would therefore be governed by air law; alternatively, they might be considered to be occurring in outer space and thus would be governed by space law. Is a reusable space plane governed by air law until it reaches Earth orbit? Or, because it is a spacecraft, does space law apply for the duration of the mission, including its transit? As a general operational rule, it can be assumed that the area where artificial satellites are able to orbit Earth qualifies as outer space, although this altitude does not necessarily reflect the ceiling of airspace. A "spatialist" approach would argue for a bright-line distinction, perhaps at 100 kilometers above the Earth's surface—often called the Kármán line.

Others first consider whether the activity involves craft with wings (like aircraft), or rockets (like spacecraft). Or they consider whether the craft takes off vertically like a rocket or horizontally like a plane. Depending on whether the craft looks like an aircraft or spacecraft, and what its mission is, it might make sense to group it under air law or space law. This "functionalist" approach does not try to decide on a physical demarcation above the Earth's surface, as the spatialist approach recommends.

Whether something qualifies as an aviation activity or a space activity impacts, and is impacted by, not only the rules of the area where it operates, but which national rules it must inherently follow and which international responsibility and liability rules apply. To date, however, no international definition has been agreed upon. This lack of certainty might be a result of the previously clear distinction between aircraft in the air and rockets and satellites in outer space. Additionally, neither the functionalist nor the spatialist approach has dominated the discussion.

As technology develops and more states and non-state actors launch different types of craft and vehicles, it may become necessary to more clearly demarcate where space begins.

A government considering space legislation might first consider whether there are any benefits to determining nationally where outer space legally begins, especially in the absence of an international definition. Likewise, a space start-up should be aware of the different regimes of air and space law, and the lack of international legal certainty between them.

Space Traffic Management

Space traffic management (STM) refers to measures taken to minimize or mitigate the negative impacts of the increasing physical congestion in space. As the number of active satellites and amount of space debris in space increases, particularly in highly used orbits and altitudes, physical congestion has become a growing problem. To date, there have been several confirmed, unintentional collisions between a functional satellite and another space object that have either damaged the satellite or completely destroyed both objects and created thousands of new pieces of space debris. The goal of STM is to try to eliminate future collisions and other incidents in space that could create additional debris or other safety risks for space activities, and to increase the safety and efficiency of space activities.

> **A government considering space legislation might first consider whether there are any benefits to determining nationally where outer space legally begins, especially in the absence of an international definition. Likewise, a space start-up should be aware of the different regimes of air and space law, and the lack of international legal certainty between them.**

Space situational awareness (SSA) is an important element of STM. SSA refers to the ability to characterize the space environment and activities in space. A key component of SSA is using ground- or space-based sensors, such as radars or optical telescopes, to track space objects. The tracking data from multiple sensors is combined to estimate orbits for space objects and predictions of their trajectories in the future. Other key components include space weather, characterization of space objects, and pre-planned maneuvers as discussed in Chapter Three: On-Orbit Operations.

While some countries currently engage in practices that could be considered to be part of STM, there currently is no widespread state practice or established international regime. In 2010, the US government began a program to provide close-approach warnings for all satellite operators. A few other countries provide similar warnings for national entities. Many satellite operators work with a third-party service, such as the Space Data Association (SDA) or their own national space agency, to augment the basic warnings and data from governments. (This is discussed more fully in Chapter Three.) There have also been international political initiatives to discuss voluntary guidelines or norms for improving the safety and sustainability of space activities, and studies to examine the interactions between space and air traffic and possible safety concerns.

There is ongoing debate over whether an international STM regime should begin with national practice or with an international treaty. Some have also made comparisons between STM and air traffic management, and called for a new treaty to establish an international body that would set standards for STM and be similar to the function of the International Civil Aviation Organization (ICAO) for air traffic management. However, ICAO was created to resolve differences between previously existing national airspace regulations. Furthermore, the air traffic standards that are set by ICAO require implementation by national regulative and administrative bodies, which many countries currently lack for space activities. As a result, others are pushing for major spacefaring states to establish national STM regimes that may evolve into an international regime in the future.

Status of Humans in Space

As states and private companies contemplate and prepare for crewed space operations ranging from suborbital to beyond Earth orbit, the legal status of humans in space within the international framework will need to be addressed. The treaty regime provides particular rights and responsibilities with regard to "astronauts," and they may or may not apply to other spaceflight participants, such as space tourists.

Article V of the Outer Space Treaty refers to astronauts as "envoys of mankind," and requires that states give them "all possible assistance in the event of accident, distress, or emergency landing" in their territory or on the high seas. This assistance also requires their safe and prompt return to the state of registry of their space vehicle. In outer space and on celestial bodies, states must render "all possible assistance" to astronauts of other states party to the treaty. Last, states must also inform other states and the UN Secretary-General of any phenomena they discover in space that could constitute a danger to the life and health of astronauts.

The 1968 Agreement on the Rescue of Astronauts, the Return of Astronauts and the Return of Objects Launched into Outer Space further develops and refines the rights and obligations of humans in space. The plain meaning of these texts is largely clear and highlights the peaceful and cooperative spirit animating the positive obligations it imposes upon states. However, neither these treaties nor any subsequent source of international law defines the term "astronaut." The issue of the status of humans in space travel is one that many new actors in space may not face immediately, but could consider in the future. It is likely that states seeking to build their space credentials will be interested in having their citizens join the list of the fewer than 600 humans who have ever traveled to outer space.

Protecting Celestial Bodies

In addition to the environmental issues discussed in previous sections, the protection of celestial bodies is an advanced issue which some new actors in space may face. Article IX of the Outer Space Treaty first establishes a positive commitment where states shall be guided by the principle of cooperation and mutual assistance, and all activities shall be conducted with due regard for the corresponding interests of other state parties. Concerning the environment of celestial bodies, all studies and exploration shall be pursued "as to avoid their harmful contamination."

The article then requires that states undertake "appropriate international consultations" before any activity or experiment they have reason to believe would cause potentially harmful interference with the space activities of other states. Last, states may request consultations concerning the activities or experiments of other states when they have reason to believe the activities or experiments would cause potentially harmful interference with their own activities.

While the text of the article is related to environmental protection, it is chiefly the second sentence of Article IX that concerns the protection of celestial bodies and creates the positive obligation for states to adopt appropriate measures to prevent the harmful contamination of outer space and celestial bodies. This sentence also concerns the creation of space debris and preventing the introduction of extraterrestrial matter to Earth. As such, this treaty article reflects the desire by states to preserve celestial bodies, and it has led to further elaboration on the meaning of planetary protection.

As mentioned, COSPAR has promulgated a Planetary Protection Policy for missions to other celestial bodies. The Planetary Protection Policy, last updated in March 2011, reflects the concerns of scientists interested in the origin of life and the preoccupation that celestial environments might be contaminated, even unintentionally, by crewed or robotic spacecraft arriving. The Planetary Protection Policy lays out five categories of missions according to the destination involved and the type of mission (i.e., orbiter, lander, return-to-Earth mission; see Table 2).

Category I missions are those to celestial bodies lacking direct relevance for understanding the process of chemical evolution or the origin of life, and include

Planetary Protection Categories		
Planetary Targets and Locations	**Mission Types**	**Mission Categories**
Undifferentiated, metamorphosed asteroids; Io; others to be determined (TBD).	Flyby, Orbiter, Lander	I
Venus; Earth's moon; Comets; non-Category I Asteroids; Jupiter; Jovian Satellites (except Io and Europa); Saturn; Saturnian satellites (except Titan and Enceladus); Uranus; Uranian satellites; Neptune; Neptunian satellites (except Triton); Kuiper-Belt Objects (< 1/2 the size of Pluto); others TBD.	Flyby, Orbiter, Lander	II+
Icy satellites where there is a remote potential for contamination of the liquid-water environments, such as Ganymede (Jupiter); Titan (Saturn); Triton, Pluto and Charon (Neptune); others TBD.	Flyby, Orbiter, Lander	II
Mars; Europa; Enceladus; others TBD (Categories IVa-c are for Mars).	Flyby, Orbiter	IIII
	Lander, Probe	IV (a-c)
Venus, moon; others TBD: "unrestricted Earth return."	Unrestricted Earth-Return	V (unrestricted)
Mars; Europa; Enceladus; others TBD: "restricted Earth return."	Restricted Earth-Return	V (restricted)

Table 2 – Planetary Protection Categories | 43

certain types of asteroids and other destinations to be determined. No planetary protection concerns are defined for Category I missions, whether they be orbiters, rovers, or landers.

Category II missions also cover orbiters, rovers, and landers, but relate to missions to several major celestial bodies: Venus, Jupiter, Saturn, Uranus, and Neptune, as well as Ganymede, Callisto, Titan, Triton, Pluto and Charon, and Ceres, as well as comets, carbonaceous chondrite asteroids, and Kuiper Belt objects. These Category II missions address missions to celestial bodies where there is a significant scientific interest related to the process of chemical evolution or the origin of life, but, because of the physical environment of the destination, there is only a remote chance that contamination might compromise future investigations. Category II missions require a record of planned impact probability and contamination control measures, as well as a documentation of the planetary protection measures taken through the general planetary protection plan, a pre-launch report, post-launch report, post-encounter report, and an end-of-mission report.

Categories III through V are for more advanced missions; either flybys or orbiters to Mars, Europa, or Enceladus (Category III), landers to Mars, Europa, or Enceladus (IV), or any Earth-Return mission (V). Earth-Return missions from Venus or the moon are classified as "Unrestricted Earth Return," while missions to and from Mars or Europa are "Restricted Earth-Return Missions" requiring heightened scrutiny.

COSPAR guidelines are implemented on a national level, where space agencies and governments adopt them into their national licensing and regulatory frameworks or implement them in the national space agency's plans. In the United States, NASA has a Planetary Protection Office, an agency-wide policy directive, and mandatory procedural requirements for its missions.

Outside of planned missions to preserve celestial bodies for their scientific value, there is also the desire to protect and preserve certain areas and artifacts on celestial bodies because of their importance to space exploration. The landing sites of the Apollo missions, including the hardware the astronauts left on the moon and even the iconic footprints from Neil Armstrong, Buzz Aldrin, and later astronauts are of permanent cultural value. The same is true for the Soviet-era rovers on the surface of the moon, such as *Lunokhod*, and of the rovers on other celestial bodies. While there has been talk of making some of these sites United Nations Educational, Scientific and Cultural Organization (UNESCO) World Heritage sites before they are encroached upon by next-generation missions, so far it is up to national governments and their space agencies to try to preserve those sites and artifacts in which they have particular interest.

For missions planned to certain destinations, responsible actors would be well-advised to educate themselves on the various planetary protection policies and to observe them in the execution of their missions.

Space Resources

As discussed at the beginning of this chapter, there are significant freedoms to explore and use outer space. The Outer Space Treaty even ensures that this exploration and use is "the province of all mankind." But what rights do states, private companies, or even people have to use space resources? While the drafters and negotiators of the Outer Space Treaty considered this topic, they left it vague enough to allow further refinement. However, this treaty—while enshrining significant freedoms in space—does have some prohibitions. Article II of the Outer Space Treaty states that:

> Outer Space, including the Moon and other celestial bodies, is not subject to national appropriation by claim of sovereignty, by means of use or occupation, or by any other means.

This article could have been made a lot shorter if it merely said "Outer Space is not subject to national appropriation," but it included extra clauses to elaborate on the negative prohibition it contains. Listing the moon and other celestial bodies shows that the prohibition applies to both physical celestial bodies and to "void" space. More importantly, the listing of claims of sovereignty, and the use of or the occupation of space, is a list of methods (or means) that would not justify a state's appropriation of outer space. Neither a statement (such as a claim) nor a physical act (such as using or occupying) constitutes lawful appropriation. Article II's list is not exhaustive; it is merely illustrative of a few explicit methods that will not legitimize national appropriation in space. Additionally, the term "celestial bodies" is nowhere defined in international law, and questions can be raised as to whether an asteroid or comet is as much a "celestial body" as one of the large planets in our solar system.

The further interpretation of this prohibition may come to the forefront as a range of activities in space become possible. Consider a situation where a crewed mission to Mars arrives at its destination after many months in space. A particular interpretation of the prohibition would indicate they are forbidden from accessing the frozen hydrogen in polar regions or the frozen waters to mix rocket fuel and create breathable air or drinkable water. According to this interpretation, all the fuel, water, and air they use on Mars must come from Earth. This is a particularly strict interpretation of the treaty and may be counter to the intended interpretation of the original drafters. The vast freedoms enshrined elsewhere in the treaty, as well as the purpose and context for which it was drafted, suggest otherwise.

An alternative interpretation suggests that use of the frozen water reserves on Mars would not qualify as national appropriation, and not be thus under the sovereign command of a nation millions of kilometers distant. Additionally, both the US and the USSR brought back lunar samples, and have acted in ways consistent with asserting and transferring uncontested ownership rights in those samples.

While the issue of the use of space resources is being examined, the purposes of the Outer Space Treaty would seem counter to overly drastic prohibitions that would limit the next generation of space activities. As long as the use of space resources conforms to the purposes of the treaty, advances the aims of the treaty, and otherwise conforms to international law, it is permissible. Additionally, as long as these activities do not rise to the level of a state establishing a sovereign appropriation akin to colonizing space or celestial bodies, they are likewise permissible.

States considering next-generation space resource activities or industries should be

States considering next-generation space resource activities or industries should be wise to consider how they will interpret their rights to use and explore space under the Outer Space Treaty, and how those rights are balanced or restricted by Article II of the Outer Space Treaty.

wise to consider how they will interpret their rights to use and explore space under the Outer Space Treaty, and how those rights are balanced or restricted by Article II of the Outer Space Treaty.

RELEVANT ORGANIZATIONS

New actors should be aware of the following organizations when conducting space activities.

International Intergovernmental Organizations

Group on Earth Observations:
Established in 2005, and currently with over 200 member countries and participating organizations, the Group on Earth Observations acts to increase interoperability between the various Earth observation systems. **www.earthobservations.org/**

Inter-Agency Space Debris Coordination Committee:
Founded in 1993, the IADC is an international governmental forum comprised of space agencies and focused on worldwide coordination of activities related to man-made and natural debris in space. The IADC formulated technical space debris mitigation guidelines. **www.iadc-online.org/**

International Committee on Global Navigation Satellite Systems:
Established in 2005, the ICG strives to promote voluntary cooperation on matters of mutual interest related to civil satellite-based positioning, navigation, timing (PNG), and value-added services. This includes coordination among providers of GNSS, regional systems, and augmentations in order to ensure greater compatibility, interoperability, and transparency. **www.unoosa.org/oosa/en/ourwork/icg/icg.html**

International Telecommunication Union:
The ITU is a specialized agency of the UN system and is based in Geneva, Switzerland. It is tasked with facilitating equitable access to the electromagnetic spectrum and orbital resources with regards to satellite services, and with promoting the advancement, implementation, and efficient operation of these services. The ITU manages the international frequency coordination process, develops global standards, and maintains the MIFR. Every three to four years, the ITU also convenes the WRC to revise or adopt the international Radio Regulations—a

treaty containing the regulatory, operational, procedural, and technical provisions applicable to radio spectra and orbital resources. Each country has one vote at the WRC, though many decisions are adopted by consensus. **www.itu.int/**

United Nations:
Established by the Charter of the United Nations in 1945, the UN is the world's largest and most important international intergovernmental political institution. Its principal organs (the General Assembly, Security Council, Economic and Social Council, Secretariat, and International Court of Justice) work to maintain international peace and security, cooperate in solving international economic, social, cultural and humanitarian problems, and promote respect for human rights and fundamental freedoms. **www.un.org/**

United Nations General Assembly:
The General Assembly is the UN's main deliberative organ, and is composed of all member states, who each have one vote on all decisions. The General Assembly meets in New York at UN Headquarters each year in the second half of September. Decisions on important matters (such as peace, security, and new members) require a two-thirds majority, while all other matters require a simple majority. Much of the work of the General Assembly is carried out by its committees and other bodies, two of which concern themselves with matters related to outer space. **www.un.org/en/ga/**

First Committee:
The First Committee of the UN General Assembly is the Disarmament and International Security committee, which tasks itself with general disarmament and international security issues which occasionally touch upon issues related to outer space. **www.un.org/en/ga/first/**

Fourth Committee:
The Fourth Committee of the United Nations General Assembly is the Special Political and Decolonization committee. The yearly report from COPUOS is received by the Fourth Committee, which also creates the mandate for the next year of work by COPUOS. **www.un.org/en/ga/fourth/**

United Nations Committee on the Peaceful Uses of Outer Space:
Established by a UN General Assembly resolution in 1958, COPUOS is the principal UN committee considering space activities. COPUOS and its two subcommittees

meet in Vienna, Austria. The Scientific and Technical Subcommittee (STSC) meets for two weeks each February, the Legal Subcommittee (LSC) meets for two weeks each March, and the large COPUOS plenary meets each June for one and a half weeks. As of 2017, membership (which is only open to states) is 84 and growing, and a diverse number of intergovernmental and non-governmental permanent observers also attend. Reports from COPUOS are sent for approval to the UN General Assembly's Fourth Committee. COPUOS is the body where the principal legal instruments, such as the Outer Space Treaty, were drafted and negotiated. **www.unoosa.org/**

United Nations Office for Outer Space Affairs:
Headquartered in Vienna, Austria, OOSA is organized under the UN Secretary-General, and has two sections: the Committee, Policy, and Legal Affairs section, and the Space Applications Section. OOSA acts as the Secretariat to COPUOS and to its two subcommittees. OOSA's Programme on Space Applications assists developing countries in using space technology for development, providing technical assistance, training, and fellowship programs in remote sensing, satellite communication, satellite meteorology, satellite navigation, space law, and basic space sciences. OOSA is also the keeper of the UN registry of space objects, and serves as the secretariat to the ICG. OOSA also manages the Platform for Space-based Information for Disaster Management and Emergency Response (UN-SPIDER) with offices in Vienna, Austria; Bonn, Germany; and Beijing, China. **www.unoosa.org/**

United Nations Conference on Disarmament:
Headquartered in Geneva, Switzerland, as a successor to previous UN-organized committees related to disarmament, the current Conference on Disarmament (CD) was established in 1980 and deals with a number of issues interrelated with disarmament, including as a regular agenda item the prevention of an arms race in outer space (PAROS). **www.unog.ch/cd**

United Nations Committee of Experts on Global Geospatial Information Management:
Established in 2011, UN-GGIM provides a forum for coordination and exchange among member states and international organizations while promoting the development of global geospatial information and its use in addressing global challenges. **http://ggim.un.org/**

World Meteorological Organization:
Established in 1950, the WMO is a specialized agency of the United Nations dedicated to international cooperation in the areas of meteorology, hydrology, and related applications. The WMO facilitates policy formulation and exchange of data related to these areas, and maintains a number of reference standards and datasets. The WMO Space Programme works to coordinate the availability and utilization of space-based data sources and products for weather and climate observation purposes in the WMO's 191 member states. **www.wmo.int**

Non-Governmental Organizations

Numerous membership based non-governmental organizations, trade associations, or other groups exist to provide industry coordination, outreach, and education functions. These entities may be domestic or international in nature and may be specific to the space and satellite sector or they may include space within a broader group of aerospace or defense industry actors. A few illustrative examples follow.

Asia-Pacific Satellite Communications Council:
The Asia-Pacific Satellite Communications Council (APSCC) is an international non-profit association representing all sectors of the satellite and/or space-related industry. Its members include satellite manufacturers, launch service providers, satellite service providers and satellite risk management companies, telecom carriers, and broadcasters from Asia, Europe and North America. APSCC's overall mission to is to promote the development and use of satellite communications and broadcasting services, as well as other aspects of space activities, for the socioeconomic and cultural welfare of the Asia-Pacific region. **http://www.apscc.or.kr/**

Commercial Spaceflight Federation:
The Commercial Spaceflight Federation (CSF) is a US-based trade organization that mainly focuses on the commercial space transportation industry. CSF was founded in 2006, and currently has more than 70 member organizations. The main goals of CSF are to promote technology innovation, guide the expansion of Earth's economic sphere, bolster US leadership in aerospace, and inspire America's next generation of engineers and explorers. **http://www.commercialspaceflight.org/**

European Association of Remote Sensing Companies:
The European Association of Remote Sensing Companies (EARSC) is a non-profit, membership based organization which promotes the use of Earth

observation technology, with an emphasis on European companies which offer Earth observation-related products and services. EARSC's mission is to foster the development of the geo-information service industry in Europe. As of December 2016 EARSC has 85 member organizations. Member of observer status is available to any organization which uses or provides remote sensing observations of the Earth and its environment, irrespective of sensor type or source (e.g. satellite, aircraft, or unmanned aerial vehicle.) **http://earsc.org/**

European, Middle-East, and Africa Satellite Operators Association:
The European, Middle-East, and Africa Satellite Operators Association (ESOA) began in 2002 as a non-profit organization representing European satellite operators, and in 2015 it expanded to cover operators in the Middle East and Africa region. ESOA's goal is to be a unified voice for global and regional satellite operators towards all international, regional, and national organisations and regulators, and achieve global coordination amongst all satellite operators across the world. **www.esoa.net**

International Amateur Radio Union:
Founded in 1925, the International Amatuer Radio Union (IARU) is an international union for the cooperation among and coordination of radio frequencies allocated to amateurs, including amateurs using amateur-satellite applications. The IARU has a Satellite Frequency Coordination division, and its IARU Satellite Advisor can help in planning space telemetry, space telecommands, and operating frequencies. Frequency coordination with the IARU is necessary in some nations for transmission from space of certain amateur allocated frequencies. **www.iaru.org/satellite.html**

International Astronautical Federation:
Founded in 1951 by scientists from around the world interested in dialogue and collaboration in the field of space research, the International Astronautical Federation (IAF) holds the yearly International Astronautical Congress (IAC) at a different locale each fall and other global conferences on space exploration, space sciences, and related themes. **www.iafastro.org/**

International Institute of Space Law:
Founded in 1960, the International Institute of Space Law (IISL) is comprised of institutions and individuals elected on the basis of their contributions to the fields of space law and related social sciences. Dedicated to fostering the development of space law, the IISL organizes and holds an annual Colloquium at the IAC in

partnership with the IAF, publishes an annual volume of its proceedings, and organizes an annual space law moot court competition and other events throughout the year. The IISL is a permanent observer at COPUOS, and in recent years has jointly organized a symposium on the first day of the COPUOS LSC meeting. **www.iislweb.org**

International Organization for Standardization:
Headquartered in Geneva, Switzerland, the ISO is an independent organization with a membership of 163 national standards bodies. Through its members, it brings together experts to share knowledge and develop voluntary, consensus-based, and market-relevant international standards that support innovation and provide solutions to global challenges. ISO maintains a standing Technical Committee on Aircraft and Space Vehicles (TC20), and subcommittees on Space Data and Information Transfer Systems (SC13) and Space Systems and Operations (SC14). **www.iso.org/**

Open Geospatial Consortium:
The OGC is a membership-based non-profit organization dedicated to the development and promulgation of open-source standards for the international geospatial community. Its members include private-sector representatives from the space, airborne, and terrestrial remote sensing industries, government agencies, academia, research organizations, and non-governmental organizations (NGOs). OGC works through a consensus process to develop standards for the interoperability and sharing of geospatial data, regardless of source. Its membership currently consists of more than 500 organizations worldwide. **www.opengeospatial.org**

Satellite Industry Association:
The Satellite Industry Association (SIA) is a US trade association representing the commercial satellite industry. SIA was formed in 1995 by several major US satellite companies as a forum to discuss issues and develop industry-wide positions on shared business, regulatory, and policy interests. SIA has established active working groups involved with a host of policy issues including government services, public safety, export control policy, international trade issues, and regulatory issues (satellite licensing, spectrum allocation, and regulatory policy). SIA is now a recognized focal point for the US satellite industry in Washington, D.C., representing and advocating industry positions with key policymakers on Capitol Hill and with the White House, Federal Communications Commission, and most Executive Branch departments and agencies. **http://www.sia.org/**

Space Frequency Coordination Group:
Comprised on member agencies including space agencies and international organizations, the SFCG works informally to develop resolutions and recommendations which express technical and administrative agreements to prevent and alleviate the risks of radiofrequency interference. The effectiveness of SFCG recommendations depends upon their voluntary acceptance and implementation by members. **www.sfcgonline.org/**

Mazlan Othman, PhD

Former Director of
the United Nations Office
for Outer Space Affairs

INTRODUCTION

A space policy and an administrative system are essential aspects of a nation's governance of its space enterprise. The authoritative structure makes possible the regulation of space actors and activities, aligning them with national development objectives and also bringing them in line with the country's international regulatory obligations.

This chapter discusses national space policy whose purpose is to define the roles and responsibilities of the different players and stakeholders. It elucidates the various components that make up the ecosystem of the space enterprise, encompassing, inter alia, investment by the private sector, interests of non-governmental entities and civil society, the foundational role of science and technology, and enforcement of controls on exports and imports.

Meanwhile, in the context of a nation's international obligations, a scheme for national oversight is necessary. The chapter brings to light the various regulators whose jurisdiction over licensing, frequency management, export controls, contracting, disputes, and liabilities should be delineated.

A case for remote sensing is presented at the end of chapter that demonstrates the necessity for the orchestration of policies and oversight.

The issues covered in this chapter are part of the plethora of a nation's undertakings in the complex management of the space enterprise. Two and a half decades ago when I initiated the Malaysian national space programme, many of these things were shrouded in secrecy and were a big mystery to me. The new entrant to the space business today will greatly benefit from the guidance provided here.

TWO   NATIONAL SPACE POLICY AND ADMINISTRATION

T his chapter provides an overview of how and why states create national frameworks for space activities through policy and regulation. A policy is a principle or a set of principles used to guide decision-making and actions.

In the context of government, "public policy" refers to why, how, and to what effect governments pursue particular courses of action or inaction. Public policy decisions often involve weighing the potential positive and negative impacts of competing options. These decisions are further complicated by the participation of many different interest groups and political actors who have competing perspectives in the decision-making process. In conjunction, "public administration" is the implementation of policy through the organization of government bureaucracy, the establishment of programs and institutions, and the day-to-day running of services and activities.

This chapter is divided into two main sections. The first section focuses on public policy aspects of national frameworks, including various ways space policy can be established; why states put in place national policy; the relationship between space and science, technology, and innovation policy; and the role of international cooperation. The second section focuses on public administration: how countries implement their own national policy and international obligations through regulative and administrative structures.

PUBLIC POLICY

Policy can be established through many different methods, several of which may be interacting at the same time. One way of establishing policy is through the international, bilateral, and multilateral treaties and agreements by which a state is bound. National policy can be established explicitly through formal decision-making processes such as intra-governmental committees or legislation. Policy can also be established implicitly through a choice to not pursue a particular path and can be manifested through cultural or ideological contexts that impact decision-making and choices. In countries with a separation between executive and legislative powers, policy may not be consistent and may even be contradictory.

In the context of space, policy can take many different forms. Some states choose to put in place a national space policy, which may or may not be accompanied by narrower policies covering specific space sectors such as launch, communications, or remote sensing. Other states choose to put in place policy at the organizational level, or through legislation that establishes specific programs and projects. Making national space policy or strategy—the documentation from the national government that spells out national goals and priorities for space—publicly accessible is one way to demonstrate intentions and priorities for a national space program. It also gives an idea of how much budgeting may go into a nation's space activities and raises the overall level of transparency. In addition, developing a national space policy or strategy forces a government to go through the process of having an intergovernmental discussion about priorities and goals for its space program, information which can then be used to inform national and international discussions. The following sections provide an overview of the different uses and common elements of space policy.

Rationales, Objectives, and Principles

A national space policy provides the rationale for why a state chooses to engage in space activities. The reasoning and motivation for engaging in space activities may differ drastically between states. Some states choose to engage in the entire spectrum of space activities and capabilities across the commercial, civil, and national security sectors, while other states chose to focus on or exclude specific types of activities. In some cases, this choice may reflect a national decision on a specific interpretation of what the peaceful uses of space means, or a state's relationship and ideological approach to its private sector. Explicitly and publicly defining the rationales for space activities may also be part of a strategy for boosting internal political support for funding and resources which support space activities.

National space policy also provides the objectives for the space activities a state chooses to engage in. The reason for doing so is to provide high-level guidance on the goals a state is pursuing. These goals can be specific, such as accomplishing a certain task in a set amount of time, or broad, such as enhancing national prestige. Explicity outlining these objectives not only provides a signal to other countries, but also can help generate national support and motivation for specific space activities and programs.

Case Study: United Arab Emirates Mars Mission

In July 2014, the government of the United Arab Emirates (UAE) announced its intentions to develop and launch a robotic spacecraft to Mars orbit. The plan marks an ambitious expansion of the UAE's space activities, which had previously focused on remote sensing and communications and coincided with the establishment of the United Arab Emirates Space Agency. The UAE's commitment to a scientific Mars exploration project encompasses many of the typical goals and drivers that are found in government space programs.

Emirati officials have described three key motivations for the project: symbolism and inspiration; acting as a catalyst for knowledge and skill development; and providing an anchor project for the domestic space industry in the UAE. The launch of the spacecraft will be symbolically important, as it is planned to arrive at Mars in 2021 to coincide with the 50th anniversary of UAE independence. The mission has also been named "Hope" with the explicit purpose of sending a message of optimism. The UAE has defined specific science objectives for the mission, and is involving local universities in the execution of scientific activities. It is planned that the spacecraft and associated mission support elements will be manufactured entirely by Emirati citizens, with up to 150 people employed in the program.

Despite the Emirati-led nature of the program, it also demonstrates the role international partnerships often play in the execution of national space programs. The spacecraft will be launched on a Japanese launch vehicle, and the government of the UAE has entered into several cooperative agreements with other nations (including the US and Russia) to exchange information related to Mars science and exploration. Through these agreements, the UAE is seeking access to training and knowledge-development for its scientists and engineers. To that end, the UAE Space Agency has also entered into an agreement with Lockheed Martin under which a training program in space-related skills will be established for students and young professionals. Although not solely related to the Mars mission, this program demonstrates the UAE's emphasis on linking space development to scientific and technical capacity-building.

National space policy can also define the principles by which a state will conduct its space activities. These principles can be used to reaffirm or demonstrate a state's adherence to international agreements and treaties, and to outline national principles that have a historical, cultural, or ideological basis. The principles in a national space policy can also form the foundation for lower-level government policies in specific sectors such as national security or commercial space.

Those proposing a new space activity in a country would be well advised to measure the compatibility of their proposal with national policy and principles related to space. If serious incompatibilities exist, strategies for overcoming them need to be addressed in the planning process.

Those proposing a new space activity in a country would be well advised to measure the compatibility of their proposal with national policy and principles related to space. If serious incompatibilities exist, strategies for overcoming them need to be addressed in the planning process.

Government Roles and Responsibilities

A second major use for national space policy is to delineate roles and responsibilities between various government agencies and entities to comply with a state's obligations under the international framework discussed in Chapter One. States need to assign responsibility to government entities performing functions such as administering and licensing radio frequencies used by communications satellites, licensing remote sensing satellites, and maintaining a national registry of space objects.

States have multiple options for how to assign roles and responsibilities. Although some countries choose to consolidate all of their space activities into one organization, it is much more common for there to be multiple government entities that are each tasked with a portion of the space activities or oversight. This division of labor could be functional, such as dividing licensing responsibilities between agencies depending on their expertise. The division could also be between civil and national security space activities, in order to enable easier public acknowledgment and international cooperation while also protecting sensitive technology or capabilities.

National space policy can also be used to direct coordination between national agencies or entities. If roles and responsibilities are divided among multiple government agencies, it is often the case that there will be a need for some of those agencies to coordinate their activities with other entities. This coordination may not happen naturally, as it can involve disputes over power, control, and budget. Space policy can be used to direct coordination with other agencies in situations where their responsibilities overlap, or direct coordination with private sector or international entities to accomplish policy objectives and principles.

The process by which a government makes national space policy decisions is important and can vary widely by country. The intra-governmental decision-making process helps ensure that space-related policies are consistent with larger policy objectives, for example foreign policy or innovation policy objectives. Decisions that are made by individual government agencies or entities without coordination and input from other stakeholders, including the private sector, are likely to be suboptimal. This is because barriers between commercial, civil, and national security space activities are increasingly becoming blurred. Most space technology is dual-use, and policy decisions on space technology need to strike a balance between controlling access to the technology to minimize national security risks and increasing access to maximize its socioeconomic benefits. As a result, policy decisions related to space activities will often result from the coordination and collaboration of the main government agencies and bodies, and may benefit from the input of advisory bodies that represent other stakeholders both within and outside of government.

For new actors in space, it is important to have administrative implementation of national policy and responsibilities. New state actors should determine how best to implement their international obligations, while also advancing their national priorities.

Although each state's national space policy is a unique reflection of its politics, culture, and priorities, there are a few common themes that occur across many national space policies. These themes reflect common challenges that states face and priorities they try to promote through their national space policies.

Role of Space in Science, Technology, and Innovation Policy

The significant socioeconomic benefits reaped by established space nations, such as the US and India, have been cited as a key motivator by emerging space countries making initial investments in space. Often tied to larger strategic goals for national science, technology, and innovation (STI) policy, space activities may include a high degree of investment in basic science and in research and development (R&D), with the goal of contributing to the national economy in sectors other than space. In this respect, a government's space policy may be a subset of STI policy, and space may be one of several other target innovation areas, such as energy, aeronautics, public health, and computing.

For new actors in space, it is important to have administrative implementation of national policy and responsibilities. New state actors should determine how best to implement their international obligations, while also advancing their national priorities.

STI policies will generally focus on the interactions among the relevant government, academic, and industry actors involved in education, basic and applied science, technology, and innovation. The coordination of STI-related efforts among the different actors is often a key challenge, as is the ability of actors within the ecosystem to integrate innovative products or processes. One particular challenge is overcoming the gap between moving from basic research to commercial adoption, sometimes referred to as the "valley of death." In this respect, STI policies will seek to not only incentivize innovation (e.g., intellectual property rules; competitive grants or awards), but also to develop the mechanisms to sustain innovation through the different development cycles so it can yield the desired economic advantages.

As an example, Mexico's National Innovation Program highlights the value of innovation in achieving sustainable economic growth and the need for policies at the federal and state levels to develop a productive innovation ecosystem. Improving the productivity and competitiveness of the manufacturing and services sectors is a main goal. With respect to space, Mexico has developed a subset of federal- and state-level policies and programs to promote innovation within this sector, such as establishing aerospace clusters to attract foreign investment and improve the competitiveness of aerospace companies in the global marketplace.

Among the primary goals often contained in STI policies is the development of a highly skilled workforce through investments in science, technology, engineering, and mathematics (STEM) education. The development of human capital is considered fundamental in industrial policy as part of efforts to develop niche capabilities and reduce the emigration of skilled or highly educated workers, also known as "brain drain." Malaysia, for example, has sought the development of a knowledge-based economy as a national political goal, a main motivator for the establishment of its national space agency. The agency is charged with realizing the vision of "harnessing space as a platform for knowledge generation, wealth creation and societal well-being." This motivation is also reflected in the practice of many countries seeking partnerships that include capacity-building components as a way to build human capital and grow national technological capacities.

Placing space activities within a larger STI framework can help answer critical questions about the long-term goals of these activities, how they relate to other science and technological efforts, and how best to coordinate among government and non-governmental efforts.

International Cooperation

International space cooperation is a key aspect of most space programs. Depending on the objectives, this cooperation can take many forms, such as multilateral cooperation at the international or regional level and bilateral cooperation with individual countries. Depending on the format of this cooperation, countries may designate specific agencies or institutions as the main representative, but the activity may involve other agencies or departments and non-governmental representatives from industry or academia.

At the multilateral level, active participation in the key space forums (e.g., the United Nations [UN] Committee on the Peaceful Uses of Outer Space [COPUOS], International Telecommunication Union [ITU]), as well as related forums for cooperation in specific application areas (e.g., the Group on Earth Observations for cooperation in Earth observation), is often considered a fundamental aspect of these activities. Countries see it as both a way to exert leadership and ensure their views are represented in relevant exchanges at the international level and a way to share information about their space activities and learn of the activities of others. This participation may thus influence policy debates at the national level.

At a regional or bilateral level, countries may adopt multiple mechanisms to formalize relationships—whether issuing joint declarations or statements, signing cooperative agreements to pursue specific activities together or to exchange data, pooling institutional or financial resources in a cooperative program, or other methods. Regional space cooperation organizations have also emerged as a way to improve cooperation in and coordination of space activities at the regional level. For example, the Asia-Pacific Regional Space Agency Forum (APRSAF) seeks to advance space activities in the Asia-Pacific region with institutions from more than 40 countries participating.

While an exhaustive description of the multiple mechanisms actors have pursued to enable international cooperation is beyond the scope of this section, the key insight is that international cooperation is rarely pursued haphazardly, but is instead often part of larger policy and strategic considerations. International cooperation is often considered both a mechanism and a goal, so it may feature in policy documents. As a mechanism, space cooperation enables actors to leverage the expertise, investments, and resources of others in the development of programs, whether through the direct acquisition of hardware or the joint development of technical capacity.

International cooperation can also be driven by larger policy objectives and be part of a strategy to advance foreign policy, innovation, or trade policy goals. In emerging space countries, the two aspects may be tightly linked. Chile's space policy, for example, identifies international space cooperation as a key initiative in efforts to advance priority areas, such as human capital and innovation. For Chile and other countries in the Latin America and Caribbean region, international cooperation—particularly bilateral and regional cooperation—is considered a priority as a way to extend limited resources, as well as to support related strategic and political goals.

Other states have pursued international space cooperation as an added measure to foster positive relationships with other countries. For example, a 2008 Policy Paper on Latin America and the Caribbean describes China's goals of engagement with countries in the region, which has included partnerships with Venezuela and Bolivia, among others.

In this respect, national space policies may detail the goals and priorities of international cooperation efforts, a mechanism that helps signal others about a government's priorities and goals in space, enhances transparency of their activities with partner nations, and invites new actors to identify opportunities for engagement.

Export Control and Technology Transfer

The underlying question when working on export controls is, with the increased access to space and burgeoning role of the private sector in space, how does a state balance controlling the proliferation of militarily-sensitive technologies with commercial development and innovation? It is particularly challenging to do so while supporting and propelling the space industrial base—an objective of many national space strategies—as export control is perceived to be a necessary part of ensuring national security and assuring a stable and predictable space environment. The balance between efficiency and commercial interests on one hand and national security on the other is a difficult one to strike; another way of looking at this is as being part of a larger discussion about promoting innovation while minimizing risks.

Keeping in mind the international aspect of export control discussed in Chapter One: Export Control, export control restrictions on the national level are extremely challenging to develop and, as a result, should be undertaken only after a considerable amount of discussion with all stakeholders, including industry, and when the government has a solid understanding of what it is trying to accomplish with export control protections. Without stakeholder input, the domestic industry can suffer unduly with very little benefit to a country's national security. States have to be careful of unintended consequences; for example, as seen in cases where export controls were changed and thus created new burdens for smaller groups in the space industry. It is important to get the conversation as wide as possible when creating government regulation about an industry, and to have an open conversation with industry to ensure that all aspects of an issue are considered.

Maintaining a list of technologies that should be controlled is challenging, particularly for space technologies, many of which are dual-use. One sticking point for export controls is that often the technology outpaces the legal regimes. This can be seen currently, for example, in regard to software development. How helpful are export regulations when they are essentially protecting outdated technology? Another significant issue is that export control, by its nature, tries to control the technology or goods themselves, regardless of how they are being used. This runs contrary to one of the emerging lessons from dealing with dual-use space technologies; it is more important to focus on the actions and use than on the technology itself.

New state actors in space should consider how they will balance their national security concerns and their position on fostering domestic industries and innovation. For non-governmental actors, a thorough appreciation of relevant export control regimes must begin early in the planning process.

New state actors in space should consider how they will balance their national security concerns and their position on fostering domestic industries and innovation. For non-governmental actors, a thorough appreciation of relevant export control regimes must begin early in the planning process.

Government Relationship with the Private Sector

Governments occupy a range of roles in their interaction with the private sector: regulator, customer, supplier (of technology and intellectual property), collaborator, and competitor. The way these roles are expressed is a major influence on the development of a broader space industry outside of the government program in a given country. Along with its role in the market as a regulator, government also exerts considerable influence through its role as a customer. Governments must be aware of how the choices they make in engaging the private sector through the procurement of goods and services affects both the development of industry and the evolution of government space strategy and programs.

Governments may choose to develop required capabilities or services internally, and not engage the private sector at all. There are several scenarios in which this approach may be preferred: the capability may not exist in the private sector, a determination might have been made that development of the capability is considered a core governmental function (for example, a capability used for national security purposes), or the capability provides a public good. Developing capabilities internally to the government provides the government with complete control over execution of the project as well as any intellectual property developed. It may help the government remain abreast of current technology, and can help government personnel stay engaged with program execution. However, in-house work has drawbacks, including a lack of transparency, and potential cost and efficiency challenges as compared to wholly private work. Governments must also remain aware of similar capabilities that the private sector may be developing in order to ensure that approaches remain current with regard to comparable capabilities.

By contracting for required capabilities, government is able to foster market competition in the private sector, which in theory supports broader economic development objectives. Competition may also lead to more innovative solutions than might be developed if the work were to be completed in-house. In general, contracting with the private sector is intended to provide capabilities in a more cost-effective and efficient manner than the developing of capabilities internally to the government. However, contracting imposes administrative costs on both the government and the private-sector entities, specifically in terms of administration and performance oversight. While typically contracts provide the government with a certain level of oversight and ability to specify quality level, contract performance attributes, and execution timelines, the contracting process inherently involves a decision to cede some control of the development of the capability, as compared to developing it in-house. Contracting may also create dependencies between the government and companies receiving contracts. The government may find itself dependent upon one or a few suppliers for a critical capability, and companies may find themselves dependent upon the government as a critical source of revenue.

Due in part to these drawbacks, governments are increasingly utilizing public-private partnership-based approaches to engage the private sector. Public-private partnership approaches typically seek to develop capabilities in a way that ensures both the government and the participating private-sector entities are co-invested in the success of the activity. Commonly, governments might specify a need and some basic requirements, as well as allocate a certain amount of funding. The capability to be acquired is one that the commercial sector can use to satisfy non-governmental requirements, with the governmental funding intended to be complemented by investment and capital provided by the commercial sector. Projects of this type give the government less control over the execution of the project but can provide capabilities at less cost than traditional contracting. The private-sector participants are required to invest their own funding. However, they are able to retain ownership of the products and intellectual property produced.

These types of activities may also be used to stimulate the development of capabilities that require governmental support to overcome initial research and development costs.

Governments may also procure capabilities on a purely commercial basis. In this approach, the private sector offers items at a standard price, commonly via a catalog. Governments are able to purchase those items in a market transaction no different from business-to-business sales. These sorts of transactions have a lower administrative burden than contracting approaches. They are typically used for the purchase of bulk goods or commodities. The government is able to procure required items quickly and efficiently but is not able to specify the details of the development process.

Governments may choose to acquire capabilities through the use of grants instead of contracts. Grants are typically used in situations where the government's interest is in acquiring research or technology development services, activities, or results. Grants provide a large amount of flexibility in execution and scope of activities and are well-suited to activities where the purpose is investigational rather than operational. Grants typically specify a topic of investigation and a general timeline for the delivery of results. They generally do not provide the government with much ability to specify performance approach or methods, nor do they require frequent reporting from awardees.

Guidance to new actors, whether they are states new to space or non-governmental private actors, is that the governmental policy toward the private or commercial space sector will have a significant impact on the business chances of those private space ventures.

Guidance to new actors, whether they are states new to space or non-governmental private actors, is that the governmental policy toward the private or commercial space sector will have a significant impact on the business chances of those private space ventures.

Case Study:
The United Kingdom Satellite Applications Catapult

The United Kingdom Satellite Applications Catapult was established by the government of the United Kingdom (UK) in May 2013 with the goal of creating economic growth in the UK through supporting the development, commercialization, and use of satellite applications. According to its Delivery Plan 2015–2020, the Catapult (Figure 8) aims to promote satellite application and technology development and to help domestic industry "bring new products and services more rapidly to market." The Satellite Applications Catapult is one of 11 "Catapults" operating in the UK, each focusing on different technologies and application areas. The Catapult operates as a private, not-for-profit research organization. It is governed by a board, which includes representation from the United Kingdom Space Agency (UKSA) and from Innovate UK—a government agency focused on fostering technology and economic development.

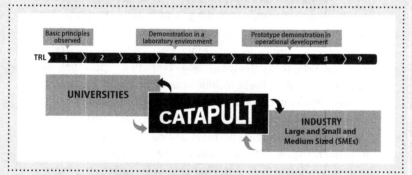

Figure 8 – The UK Satellite Applications Catapult
Source: Adapted from Satellite Applications Catapult Peterborough Industry Day Presentation, February 2015.

The UK-wide Catapult network was established to promote innovation and improve the ability of UK industry to commercialize outputs from what the government viewed as a strong national fundamental research capacity. In November 2014, the UK government published the UK Space Innovation and Growth Strategy Growth Action Plan. This plan set a target of growing the annual revenue of the UK space industry from

£11.3 billion as of October 2014 to £40 billion by 2030. The Satellite Applications Catapult has since been positioned as one of several policy strategies the UK government is employing as components of achieving this revenue target.

The Catapult views increasing exports as a key element of achieving this growth. To this end, its programs support the development of satellite applications-based products. The Catapult focuses its efforts on working with companies (and academia) to bridge what is known as the "valley of death" in the process of transferring a product or technology from fundamental research to active commercialization. The "valley of death" refers to the gap in available funding and resources that developers often encounter between the fundamental research phases of development and the commercialization phase.

The Catapult is not a funding agency itself—it does not provide direct grants or financing to industry (or academia). Instead, it acts as a technical, networking, and facilities resource for UK companies looking to develop and commercialize satellite applications. The Catapult maintains technical facilities, including labs, test equipment, and computing capabilities, at its central campus. These facilities can be accessed and rented for development purposes. The organization regularly hosts business networking workshops and events and works to link UK businesses to foreign partners and business opportunities. It actively helps UK companies raise private capital and maintains relationships with finance sources such as the Space Angels Network. The Catapult also helps UK companies identify intellectual property and human capital resources related to their business objectives. The Catapult may also partner with companies to pursue specific business opportunities, jointly developing satellite applications projects in response to available funding sources.

Property Rights

Ownership and control rights to space objects launched by a state and registered by it are protected for that state (and are protected for its nationals as long as their state extends those rights to them). These rights may also apply to a state that procures a launch from another country. Other tangible property rights are more uncertain.

There is, for example, no clearly identified mechanism in international law for the transfer of jurisdiction to a non-launching state in the case of a satellite sale or transfer. Registering states are usually also launching states. De-registration from one state registry and subsequent re-registration on a new state registry would seem to be the only available path to clearly and transparently transfer national jurisdictional competency. Chapter One: Registration of Space Objects, and the sub-section on United Nations General Assembly (UNGA) 62/101, show a path forward for this.

Concerning rights to resources, while samples of space materials may be obtained, commercial rights to extracted natural resources in space are widely debated and, so far, untested. Since the Outer Space Treaty prohibits claims to sovereignty over any celestial body, states are effectively prohibited from granting title to any real property beyond Earth. States retain jurisdiction over their nationals, however, and this means that states have the power to protect the commercial operations of their nationals from interference from others with the same nationality. This is the strategy employed by the US in crafting its US Commercial Space Launch Competitiveness Act of 2015.

The debate over rights to material extracted from a celestial body is complicated by differences over the meaning of the ban on "appropriation" in the Outer Space Treaty. For some, that means a prohibition on assuming any property right for off-Earth material. For others, there is a clear distinction between the use of resources extracted or harvested from a celestial body, such as regolith or water, and ownership of the body itself. Since the United States, Russia, and Japan have all obtained material from celestial bodies, returned it to Earth, and exercised full ownership and control of it, any ban is shown by practice to not be absolute.

For the immediate future, then, it appears that property rights to material obtained from celestial bodies will largely be determined by national legislation, and that those rights will pertain only within the territorial and personal jurisdiction of the legislating state. As a cautionary note, business plans developed with the intention of exporting off-Earth material or products derived from it should ensure that the sovereigns with authority over the intended export markets will permit the sale of such material and products. No rules specific or unique to space activity exist for intellectual property. In general terms, the rules are the same as those that would apply for terrestrial activity.

PUBLIC ADMINISTRATION AND NATIONAL OVERSIGHT

As explained in the previous chapter, states bear international responsibility and liability for damage caused by the space activities of their nationals. They also are tasked with oversight of their national space activities, including space activities conducted by non-governmental actors. States use national legislation and regulations to fulfill these international legal obligations. In accordance with their policy rationales and objectives, as discussed previously in this chapter, a number of domestic administrative methods or levers exist by which governments exercise oversight of both government and non-governmental space activities.

National Regulators

The Outer Space Treaty obligates state parties to authorize, license, and continually supervise national activities for conformity with international law, but it is at the discretion of each state's government to determine which agencies are tasked with this regulation. In some countries, these responsibilities will be divided among several different agencies.

In the United States, for example, the Federal Aviation Administration (FAA) has responsibility for commercial launches, the Federal Communications Commission (FCC) deals with telecommunications and frequency allocations, the National Oceanic and Atmospheric Administration (NOAA) regulates remote sensing, and the Department of State and the Department of Commerce share responsibility for export control. Deciding which agency is covering which activity can eliminate both gaps and redundancies in the oversight regime.

Deciding which agency is covering which activity can eliminate both gaps and redundancies in the oversight regime.

Licensing

Licensing is the standard method used by a state to authorize and regulate its national, non-governmental space activities. Individual actors must comply with requirements to obtain national licenses before undertaking space activities. The types of licenses required can vary: launch licenses, frequency-use licenses, remote sensing licenses, broadcasting licenses, etc. The criteria for obtaining these licenses can include scientific, technical, environmental, safety, insurance, and financial solvency requirements, to name a few. In most cases, private sector space activities require positive confirmation (i.e. a license) before they are allowed to occur. This is different from many non-space sectors, where private sector activities are often allowed by default, and only specific types of activities, for example those that are particularly risky or harmful, are required to have permission to proceed.

> **Understanding the licensing requirements in the applicable jurisdiction is incredibly important to successful and responsible space operations.**

Understanding the licensing requirements in the applicable jurisdiction is incredibly important to successful and responsible space operations.

National Registries of Space Objects

In accordance with the Outer Space Treaty and the Registration Convention, states assert ownership of their space objects by placing them on their national registries. This ownership is twofold, encompassing jurisdiction and control. Jurisdiction is a legal power to create and enforce laws and to settle claims, and is held by the state. Control is an operational power analogous to command over the space object. Article VIII of the Outer Space Treaty confers these rights:

> *A State Party to the Treaty on whose registry an object launched into outer space is carried shall retain jurisdiction and control over such object, and over any personnel thereof, while in outer space or on a celestial body. Ownership of objects launched into outer space, including objects landed or constructed on a celestial body, and of their component parts, is not affected by their presence in outer space or on a celestial body or by their return to Earth. Such objects or component parts found beyond the limits of the State Party to the Treaty on whose registry they are carried shall be returned to that State Party, which shall, upon request, furnish identifying data prior to their return.*

While the Outer Space Treaty gives states the rights and the method to assert jurisdiction and control, it does not make it mandatory; the 1975 Registration Convention, in turn, requires and obligates states to establish national registries of space objects. For states party to the Registration Convention, Article II requires the establishment of a national registry, and providing notification of the establishment of such registry to the UN Secretary-General.

National registries are usually created through legislative acts, either as part of general space legislation or in an act specifically for the purpose of creating such a registry, as in the cases of Argentina, the Netherlands, and Italy. National registries may also be created by executive decree or within regulations by an agency granted the power to create them.

As of 2017, 63 states were party to the 1975 Registration Convention, and 31 of them had established national registries of space objects and informed the UN of such national registries. European Space Agency (ESA) and European Organisation for the Exploitation of Meteorological Satellites (EUMETSAT) have also established registries. Table 3 lists national registries of space objects, and which governmental agencies maintain its national registry. Some states place the task with their national space agency, others with their federal aviation office even if they have a national space agency, as is the case with Germany.

For states wishing to exercise jurisdiction and control over space objects, establishing and maintaining a national registry of space objects is a reliable method to assert and consolidate jurisdictional powers. It might also be the state's duty to establish and maintain such a registry. For non-governmental actors, due diligence and compliance with governmental oversight likely includes determining which state will have their spacecraft on its national registry and supplying that agency with the relevant information on their spacecraft and activity.

> **For states wishing to exercise jurisdiction and control over space objects, establishing and maintaining a national registry of space objects is a reliable method to assert and consolidate jurisdictional powers.**

National Registries of Space Objects			
State	**OST**	**REG**	**Agency Maintaining the National Registry**
Argentina	✓	✓	National Commission on Space Activities of Argentina (CONAE)
Australia	✓	✓	Space Licensing and Safety Office of the Government of Australia
Austria	✓	✓	Ministry of Transport, Innovation and Technology
Belarus	✓	✓	National Academy of Sciences (NASB)
Belgium	✓	✓	Belgian Science Policy Office (BELSPO)
Brazil	✓	✓	Brazilian Space Agency (AEB)
Canada	✓	✓	Canadian Space Agency (CSA)
Chile	✓	✓	Ministry of Foreign Affairs–Directorate for International and Human Security
China	✓	✓	China National Space Administration (CNSA)
Czech Republic	✓	✓	Czech Ministry of Transport
France	✓	✓	National Center for Space Studies (CNES)
Germany	✓	✓	Federal Aviation Office (LBA)
Greece	✓	✓	Ministry for Foreign Affairs of Greece
India	✓	✓	Department of Telecommunications– Wireless and Planning Coordination Wing
Italy	✓	✓	Italian Space Agency (ASI)
Japan	✓	✓	Ministry of Education, Sports, Culture, Science and Technology (MEXT)
Kazakhstan	✓	✓	Ministry for Investment and Development– Aerospace Committee (KazCosmos)
Mexico	✓	✓	Mexican Space Agency–General Coordination Office for Space-Related Security and International Affairs
Netherlands	✓	✓	Ministry of Economic Affairs Telecommunications Agency
North Korea	✓	✓	National Aerospace Development Administration
Norway	✓	✓	Norwegian Space Center (NSC)
Pakistan	✓	✓	Pakistan Space and Upper Atmosphere Research Commission (SUPARCO)
Peru	✓	✓	National Aerospace Research and Development Center (CONIDA)
Russia	✓	✓	State Space Corporation (Roscosmos)
Slovakia	✓	✓	Department of Higher Education, Science and Research– Ministry of Education, Science, Research and Sport
South Africa	✓	✓	Department of Trade and Industry– South Africa Council for Space Affairs
South Korea	✓	✓	Ministry of Science, Information and Communications Technology, and Future Planning (MSIP)
Spain	✓	✓	Ministry of Foreign Affairs– Department of International Economic Relations
Ukraine	✓	✓	National Space Agency of Ukraine (NSAU)
UK	✓	✓	UK Space Agency (UKSA)
USA	✓	✓	Department of State–Bureau of Oceans and International Environmental and Scientific Affairs

NATIONAL SPACE POLICY AND ADMINISTRATION

Table 3 – National Registries of Space Objects

Insurance Requirements

In order to ensure that entities undertaking space activities are able to indemnify the state in case international liability is incurred, and/or are able to pay claims by fellow nationals, many states require entities engaging in space activities to carry insurance. After R&D costs and launch costs, insurance is typically the third-highest cost associated with satellite activities, and thus is something to seriously consider when planning for a space venture. For example, Australia, Brazil, France, Japan, South Korea, the UK, and the US all require the purchase of insurance at varying levels, as shown in Table 4.

Waivers

There are different kinds of waivers that may be used for space activities. A cross-waiver is a legal instrument between parties where each reciprocally contracts to not hold the other party liable for any damage suffered. Cross-waivers of liability are often used in the space industry and might be used between the launch provider and the operator, and also between contractors and sub-contractors. Waivers have the effect of making it easier to contemplate and compute the possible liability exposure a project faces.

On a regulatory level, waivers can be granted in order to relieve operators from following a regulation that evolved after their satellite was launched. This type of waiver might also be called a "variance." Alternatively, operators can apply for a waiver from obeying a regulation that they believe to be unduly onerous or to have national security consequences. Granting waivers can be used by regulators to allow an industry to innovate.

National Frequency Administration and Broadcasting

The International Telecommunication Union deals with frequency allocation and coordination at the international level, which is covered in Chapter One: International Frequency Management. National administrators determine frequency use at the domestic level, commonly through licensing and national frequency tables. For example, the Ministry of Communications and Information Technology in India handles their national frequency allocations, and the Office of Communications (Ofcom) in the UK provides licenses for radiofrequency use. In the United States, the FCC coordinates non-federal use of frequencies, while the National Telecommunications and Information Administration (NTIA) coordinates federal spectrum use.

Indemnification Regime of Some Spacefaring States			
Country	Regime	Third-Party Liability Amount	Comments
Australia	Space Activities Act of 1998	A$750 million or Maximum Probable Loss	Limit up to A$3 billion for claims by Australian nationals
Brazil	Resolution on Commercial Launching Activities from Brazilian Territory (Res. No. 51 of 26 January 2001); Regulation on Procedures and on Definition of Necessary Requirements for the Request, Evaluation, Issuance, Follow-up and Supervision of Licenses for Carrying out Launching Space Activities on Brazilian Territory (No. 27)	(no fixed amount)	
France	Space Operations Act of 2008 (entered into force 10 December 2010)	€60 Million	
Japan	Law Concerning Japan Aerospace Exploration Agency, Law Number 161 of 13 December 2002	¥20 billion for H-IIA; ¥5 billion for smaller rocket (e.g., Epsilon)	Amount of the insurance depends on the specific launch vehicle
South Korea	Space Liability Act (Republic of Korea) Law n. 8852 of 21 December 2007	KRW200 billion maximum	
United Kingdom	Outer Space Act 1986, as amended 1 October 2015	€60 Million	Operator third-party liability limited to maximum of €60M for cases "involving single satellite missions employing established launchers, satellite platforms and operational profiles"
USA	US Code Chapter 509– Commercial Space Launch Activities	Up to $500 million based on per-mission Maximum Probable Loss calculation	Any claims exceeding the insured amounts are payable by the US government on behalf of the licensee, up to the statutory maximum of $1.5 billion (subject to congressional appropriation)

Table 4 – Indemnification Regime of Some Spacefaring States

In addition to working on frequency issues, these administrators can reinforce other best practices. For example, in order to receive authorization from the FCC to use a frequency, US commercial satellite operators must submit an orbital debris mitigation plan that is in accordance with internationally recognized debris mitigation guidelines. Laws and regulations pertaining to broadcasting are not limited only to space-based services and can include other sectors such as cable television. It is important for any entity undertaking space-based broadcasting activities to comply with any relevant national rules regarding broadcasting generally. For example, in Canada, companies engaged in broadcasting are required to broadcast a certain amount of Canadian content. The national regulator may also impose resolution limitations on remote sensing or limitations on power emissions.

Spectrum regulation is a part of a government's responsibility for oversight. This planning function allows for spectrum allocation, which grants use of a frequency band to a specific user, dependent upon national policies, technical characteristics of the spectrum, and international agreements. This allocation process helps ensure that the spectrum is managed and used in a sustainable way while limiting the amount of harmful interference created by its use. Next, spectrum engineering is the regulatory function that creates technical standards for equipment whose frequencies affect or are affected by the radio spectrum. Finally, there is spectrum compliance, which involves monitoring the use of the radiofrequency spectrum to ascertain that users are complying with technical standards and frequency allocations.

Administration of Export Controls and Technology-Transfer
States implement export control measures to meet international commitments for non-proliferation regimes, to enhance regional stability, and out of national security interests. States must decide how to administer export control laws.

In order to reliably control exports, a country must establish legal authority to do so, which would correspond to six principles: comprehensive controls, implementing directives, enforcement power and penalties, interagency coordination, international cooperation, and protection of government dissemination of sensitive business information. Next, a country needs to establish clear regulatory procedures that include a list of controlled items. Finally, the export control system should have enforcement built into it, including transparent procedures for issuing export licenses, compliance mechanisms, and investigation of possible illicit exports.

Case Study: Export Controls in the United States

The US has three agencies with the authority to issue export control licenses: the Departments of Commerce, State, and the Treasury. Often, exporters must go to more than one agency and must ask for multiple licenses. There is interest in streamlining this process to have one single licensing agency in charge, although this would be a complicated effort and challenging to implement.

The US Department of State administers perhaps the most well-known example of export control regimes, the International Traffic in Arms Regulations (ITAR), a set of US government regulations that control the export and import of defense-related articles and services on the US Munitions List (USML). Businesses must register their products with the State Department's Directorate of Defense Trade Controls (DDTC), and are required to apply for export licenses and approvals for hardware on the USML or technical data that can be exported. The process can be expensive and lengthy and can add significant burden to commercial activities, particularly for smaller firms. Failure to comply with the ITAR requirements can lead to serious fines, jail time, and other civil and criminal penalties.

Satellites and related technologies present a significant challenge for export control. In the early 2000s, US Congress passed legislation that placed all satellites and space-related technologies on the USML, due to concerns over transfer of space technology to China that could be used to improve ballistic missiles. The stricter controls on export of US satellite technology led to foreign firms developing their own products, which were often marketed as "ITAR-free." As a result, the global market share for US satellite companies dropped precipitously. A strong push from industry led to Congress passing an updated law in 2012 that gave the White House the authority to determine which specific space technologies would remain on the USML, and which technologies would be transferred to the less onerous Commercial Control List (CCL), while retaining a prohibition on export of space technologies to specific countries. In 2014, after two years of interagency and public deliberations, the Department of Commerce announced the shift of some types of satellites and space technologies to the CCL.

However, the steps to reform US export controls for satellites have not satisfied all the critics. Companies now need to determine whether or not they need to apply for a license from the State Department or the Commerce Department, and the overall system has become more complex. Furthermore, commercial satellites performing above a certain standard would still remain on the USML, as would any spacecraft designed for human habitation that has integrated propulsion. There continues to be an on-going discussion between the US space industry and the US government over future changes and reforms to export control.

Congestion in Space

As states are responsible for their own space activities and those of their non-governmental entities, national policies and administration for dealing with congestion in space are important for improving space sustainability. Efforts to tackle the problem of congestion fall into three major categories, with each category addressing a different aspect of the problem: limiting the creation of new space debris, addressing the legacy population of space debris already in orbit, and minimizing the negative impact of the existing debris on space activities.

Case Study: Space Debris Policy and Administration in the United States

In the United States, the national space policy directs all federal agencies to adhere to the US Government Orbital Debris Mitigation Standard Practices, which closely reflect the Inter-Agency Space Debris Coordination Committee (IADC) guidelines. The standard practices apply to all US governmental programs and projects, including those directly carried out by US agencies and those funded by the US government. The various federal agencies that conduct governmental space activities each have their own policy guidance and framework for implementing these directives. There are some parts of the implementation that are coordinated through the interagency process, but also some parts that are left to agency discretion.

There are also three US federal agencies with existing regulatory authority over non-governmental space activities that implement and enforce space debris mitigation guidelines on the private sector. NOAA under the Department of Commerce has the authority to license non-governmental space-based remote sensing of Earth. The FAA under the Department of Transportation has licensing authority over commercial launch, re-entry or reusable vehicles, commercial launch or re-entry facilities, and commercial human spaceflight. The FCC also has the authority to provide licenses to the radio frequency spectrum for non-governmental satellite activities.

In general, the space debris mitigation guidelines are currently implemented for non-governmental space activities as part of the licensing processes in each of these three agencies. However, there are differences in the requirements set by these agencies. For example, the FCC requires that licensees present a plan for debris mitigation during both normal operations and post-mission disposal, whereas NOAA requires that licensees present a plan for just post-mission disposal of their remote sensing satellite. The FCC also requires licensees to follow the 25-year rule in de-orbiting all pieces from a space launch, whereas the FAA does not. These differences in licensing requirements and rules are largely due to the differences the two agencies have in their approach to risk mitigation as a result of different legislative and policy mandates. Furthermore, only NOAA currently has regulatory authority over operational space activities—the other two entities conduct pre-launch licensing and certification only.

A topic many states struggle with is potential exceptions to the space debris mitigation guidelines. It may be necessary to exempt some long-running government programs from specific aspects of the guidelines because portions of the program(s) were designed and implemented before the guidelines were adopted. States may also be inclined to exempt some new programs over concerns that implementing the guidelines will lead to increased costs or operational challenges. However, widespread exemptions would have a deleterious effect on adherence to the guidelines, which would ultimately negatively impact all space actors. If states are to make exemptions to the guidelines, they should do so through a well-defined, rigorous process that includes high-level decision-makers and clearly outlines the costs and benefits of the exemptions.

In addition to limiting the creation of new debris, several states have also put in place policies and administrative practices to minimize the impact that existing space debris have on space activities. The United States, Russia, France, Germany, and Japan are among the states that have governmental organizations tasked with monitoring the population of space objects and predicting potential close approaches. In some cases, these organizations do so for their own governmental satellites, while in others they do so for non-governmental or foreign satellites as well. In either case, they have put in place procedures and data-sharing mechanisms for notifying satellite operators and assisting them in assessing the risk of collision and implementing any avoidance measures.

These practices are often included in the larger discussion about space traffic management (STM), but at present there is no standard national practice for implementing STM in a comprehensive manner. It is currently up to each satellite operator to determine their own tolerance for risk and to use that as a basis for determining whether to take steps to avoid a close approach with another space object. Current techniques for predicting close approaches and possible collisions in orbit are not sophisticated enough to enable mandatory maneuver policies, with the specific exception of activities such as human spaceflight.

Several states have also put in place policies and organizations for providing a national space situational awareness (SSA) capability. Developing the capability to track all space objects requires a considerable network of tracking-station locations around the world. Thus, most countries focus on developing a more limited national capability over their own territory. In most cases, it is either based on existing national military or intelligence capabilities or dual-use capabilities. This can create challenges for states that do not have a prior working relationship between their national security community and their civil space community, or for states that try to develop SSA capabilities as a purely civil function.

An example of how to overcome this challenge can be seen in the case of Germany. The Federal Ministry for Economic Affairs and Energy is the lead entity for space affairs in Germany and coordinated the process of establishing a German national space strategy. The coordination involved the German Aerospace Center (DLR), which is responsible for the execution of the national space program, and the Federal Ministry of Defence, which operates several satellites. Part of the implementation of the strategy was the creation of the German Space Situational Awareness Center, a joint venture between the DLR and the German Air Force, in 2009.

All states are encouraged to put in place national mechanisms to implement the IADC Space Debris Mitigation Guidelines for both governmental and non-governmental actors. How they are implemented can vary depending on a state's specific governmental structure. Usually, implementation includes policy directives for federal agencies, a regulatory component in national law, and licensing requirements for non-governmental entities.

All states are encouraged to put in place national mechanisms to implement the IADC Space Debris Mitigation Guidelines for both governmental and non-governmental actors. How they are implemented can vary depending on a state's specific governmental structure.

Government Contracting

Governments commonly contract for the delivery of required goods and/or services from private sector enterprises. Contracts, which take various forms (see Table 5), generally specify technical and performance requirements for the goods or services to be delivered, a timeline for execution, performance reporting requirements, and financial terms of payments. In general, contracts are intended to pay for the cost of developing and delivering a required capability, along with a certain amount of profit or fee for the company executing the work.

Dispute Settlement Clauses

In contracting, parties will likely desire to place particular clauses for the predictable and fair settlement of disputes. The Model Law on International

Common Contract Types	
Fixed Price	Specific, exact price for services and delivery terms; maximizes incentive for contractor to control costs; reduces government insight into performance; reduces incentives for innovation.
Cost Reimbursement	Costs are variable based on expenses incurred and fee rate; little incentive for contractor to control costs; potential for scope overruns; high degree of government insight into performance.
Time and Materials	Costs are variable based on expenses incurred and fee rate; difficult to manage the amount of work performed; best-suited for highly defined scopes.

Table 5 – Common Contract Types

Commercial Arbitration, drafted by the United Nations Commission on International Trade Law (UNCITRAL), defines the principal requirements, or elements, of dispute resolution by arbitration. These principles might be included in an international agreement. The principal requirement is an agreement by the parties to submit to arbitration all (or certain) disputes which have arisen or which may arise out of a defined legal relationship between them, whether the disputes are contractual or not.

Only claims arising out of a defined legal relationship are covered by the arbitration agreement. Generally, the agreement will refer to claims "which arise out of or in connection with this contract." Such language is sufficient to encompass all issues associated with the contract's conclusion, validity, interpretation, performance, damages, and termination. Tort claims may be covered if they bear some nexus to the performance of the parties' relevant contractual obligations.

Finally, there are the Optional Rules for Arbitration of Disputes Relating to Outer Space Activities, which have been put forth by the Permanent Court of Arbitration (PCA). As discussed in Chapter One: Arbitration and Mediation, these rules provide sample arbitration clause language that can be used in instances where the parties wish to implement the Optional Rules. If the parties agree to refer a dispute to the PCA under these Optional Rules, then a "waiver of any right to immunity from jurisdiction, in respect of the dispute in question, to which such party might otherwise be entitled" will be construed; it would not be necessary for a jurisdiction to characterize the dispute as specifically relating to outer space for these rules to apply. The Optional Rules are based on and modify the 2010

UNCITRAL Arbitration Rules and are meant to address the particular needs of parties engaging in space activities. They contain the relevant language to govern elements of arbitration, including notice, representation, number and selection of arbitrators, and procedures to be followed.

Recourse to Domestic Courts

Of course, in a commercial dispute, recourse to domestic courts is an option in any court that would possess jurisdiction over the dispute in accordance with its rules. Whether or not a state can be party to a dispute in a domestic court, though, will be a separate question. Issues such as sovereign immunity play a role in whether a court will be considered to have jurisdiction over a particular state. The key threshold question with regard to pursuit of any case in domestic court is jurisdiction, both over the parties and over the subject matter. When jurisdiction has been determined, then a plaintiff must consider the most favorable forum in which to pursue the claim. Such issues as access to enforcement mechanisms for a judgment, in addition to consideration of prior case law in the jurisdiction, should be considered before selecting a forum.

IN-DEPTH ANALYSIS: REMOTE SENSING POLICY AND ADMINISTRATION

Remote sensing satellites have continually sensed Earth for more than four decades, yielding a valuable repository of data about the planet which has applications in areas as far-reaching as health, climatology, and urban planning. Given its strong linkages to socioeconomic development, space-based remote sensing is a key area of activity for new and established space actors alike. In light of this, remote sensing is a useful case study highlighting the interaction between public policy and public administration and illustrates some of the approaches different countries have taken to managing this kind of activity. Additionally, new trends in remote sensing activities, especially by non-governmental actors, illustrate larger policy transformations that are useful for new space actors to consider.

Remote Sensing Policy

Consistent with the main elements of public policy described in the beginning of this chapter, remote sensing policies primarily seek to:

- identify objectives and priorities guiding the acquisition of data about the planet;

- define roles and responsibilities of government remote sensing activities as well as related oversight obligations;
- set requirements by designating procedures private operators must follow to operate remote sensing systems; and
- identify data policies to govern the conditions of access and distribution of the data acquired through the operation of these systems.

Remote sensing policies may be included within national-level space policies or may have dedicated policies of their own. In some cases, a government will lay out specific goals with respect to the information being collected or priority application areas, identifying departments or agencies that are responsible for acquiring research or operational datasets. Specific government agencies may also be tasked with operating specific systems. Sector guidance in the 2010 US National Space Policy, for example, dictates that the US Geological Survey (USGS) and National Aeronautics and Space Administration (NASA) shall cooperate to maintain an operational land remote sensing program. The policy also describes tasks related to the acquisition, archiving, and distribution of the global land remote sensing dataset.

In light of technological advances driving the proliferation of these systems and the international liability responsibilities discussed in Chapter One, remote sensing policies also define roles with respect to the oversight of non-governmental remote sensing activities, identifying the specific department or agency and the tasks they perform in the process. These guidelines may be further detailed in related regulations, laws, or agency-level policies. In the United States, the licensing authority of private remote sensing space systems lies with the Secretary of Commerce, a task that has been delegated to the NOAA for implementation, and whose principles are captured in a national Commercial Remote Sensing Policy. NOAA agency-level policies specify the principles guiding related activities, such as a partnership policy among government, academia, and the private sector in the provision of environmental information and services.

Policies also allude to coordination processes necessary to orchestrate the different elements involved in managing remote sensing activities, which, in addition to the those common for any satellite mission (research, development, launch, operations, etc.), include tasks specific to the processing, archiving, and distribution of Earth observations data. Institutional coordination is particularly necessary in the field of remote sensing because of the diversity of users and stakeholders who routinely derive valuable intelligence from this information. Understanding needs across these different user communities is an often challenging but crucial task that feeds into this coordination process to improve the value of investments in remote sensing programs.

Oversight of Non-Government Activities

Rapid technological advances often drive the evolution of remote sensing policies, particularly given the growth of high-resolution imaging satellites from non-governmental sources. Remote sensing policies primarily seek to advance national (including commercial) remote sensing activities for the provision of services, imagery/data or value-added products while balancing national security and foreign policy interests. To do this, the policy will specify procedures that non-governmental operators must meet to be allowed to operate space remote sensing systems, and the limitations on such activities. Access to the data acquired by these systems, whether freely or commercially, is also subject to specific limitations imposed by the oversight authority. Canada's Remote Sensing Space Systems Act of 2005, for example, details the procedure by which an operational license may be cancelled or temporarily revoked when it is determined to be "injurious to national security, the defence of Canada, the safety of Canadian Forces or Canada's conduct of international relations" or "inconsistent with Canada's international obligations." In some countries, a license may not be revoked but the operator may be required to temporarily cease operations during crisis or conflict—sometimes called "shutter control"—or to refrain from sensing or distributing data on areas of the world deemed to be sensitive by the licensing authority.

Permissions are often granted through licenses issued after the operator has committed to meeting certain operational and even disposal procedures, and sometimes following inter-agency review. As an example, a US commercial remote sensing license application available on the NOAA Commercial Remote Sensing Regulatory Affairs website highlights the basic requirements, including the following:

- **Corporate information:** contact information and other details about the business, a description of significant agreements with foreign nations or persons, etc.
- **Launch segment information:** proposed launch schedule, anticipated operational date, orbital parameters, etc.

- **Space segment information:** anticipated resolution and swath width of sensors, on-board storage capacity, anticipated system lifetime, etc.
- **Ground segment information:** proposed system data collection and processing capabilities, transmission frequencies, plans for protection of uplink and downlink, etc.
- **Other information** including financial information about proposed commercial data distribution policies, a plan for post-mission satellite disposal, etc.

Data Policies

Data policies are a key component of remote sensing policies since these specify the access and distribution rights and obligations of data acquired through these activities. Generally, policies make most government-acquired remote sensing datasets available for scientific, social, and economic benefit by making the data available to users across government, academia, and the private sector. The European Union's Copernicus system's data policy "promotes the access, use and sharing of Copernicus information and data on a full, free, and open basis," and is specifically tied to the promotion of economic development and technological innovation goals. Bilateral and multilateral data exchange programs also exist to facilitate the sharing of specific datasets among operators and users of partner countries or when such exchange helps address shared challenges. The World Meteorological Organization (WMO), for example, facilitates the international exchange of meteorological and related data and products, including those derived from space-based systems, as tied to "matters relating to safety and security of society, economic welfare and the protection of the environment." National open-data policies may also apply, usually as part of a larger policy governing the access and use of government-funded data that is not limited to space, and may include data acquired through airborne or *in-situ* platforms.

Even with the proliferation of open data access policies, remote sensing policies include language specifying conditions of restriction on access or redistribution of datasets, particularly driven by national security concerns. The main driver for these different policy elements is the inherent dual-use nature of remote sensing technologies, which enable applications across civil, commercial, and military domains. In some countries, such as Chile, a single remote sensing satellite or system serves the needs of both civil and military users, thus making it "dual use." However, even while a satellite or a system may be designed to serve exclusively civil needs, the dual-use nature of the technology remains, as the data gathered can be aggregated or reused to feed into applications for military purposes. Consequently, and to balance national security concerns associated with access to potentially sensitive information, data policies typically specify resolution or temporal restrictions for the distribution of high-resolution data or imagery, including those from commercial operators and providers. The exchange or redistribution of these datasets may be subject to additional requirements and examined on a case-by-case basis. In Germany, Earth observation data acquired through "high-grade" systems are subject to the German National Data Security Policy for Space-Based Earth Remote Sensing Systems, and distribution is allowed depending on the level of "sensitivity" of the data. Moreover, India's Remote Sensing Data Policy of 2011 notes that specific agreements are necessary for the exchange of data better than 1-meter resolution.

Broader Policy Context

Driven in large part by technological advances, data policies—and their application through licenses and other legal mechanisms—will remain a focal point in the evolution of remote sensing practice currently manifest through the emergence of multiple sources of non-government data and services. The expansion of non-government actors in the full value-chain of remote sensing activity—from research and operations to data processing and archiving—is one of the trends raising new policy and regulatory questions. Another important trend is the proliferation of geospatial products and services that result from the aggregation of multiple datasets, which may come from several data providers and are often collected from various space-based, airborne, and *in-situ* platforms. In a context where space activities represent a portion of the remote sensing activities that governments must oversee, space-derived data and services may be subject to regulation or oversight by multiple government agencies and be governed under different legal regimes. For example, privacy debates arising from uninhabited aircraft systems (UAS) in the US are beginning to expand to include discussion of similar concerns related to small satellites, despite the fact that these systems currently operate in distinct legal domains. These and other developments suggest that in some countries, new rules may emerge that apply to applications or the kinds of data being collected, rather than specific collection platforms. In this context, new space actors should be aware of this broader policy context and should pay attention to how public administration practices—encompassing policy, legal, and regulatory measures—from non-space domains may apply to this key area of space activities.

Greg Wyler
Founder and
Executive Chairman
OneWeb

INTRODUCTION

E arth orbit offers a unique vantage for critical applications in industry, science, policy, and more. Historically, many have thought this space real estate was virtually infinite; however, with satellite constellations, we will fast approach the congestion limits of various orbits.

Operators may use these orbits, but, like other environmental resources, they must protect them for future generations. Spacecraft, constellation, and operational design should minimize the chance of creating debris during both the active mission lifetime and the disposal phase of the spacecraft. Perhaps industry will align on voluntary norms of behavior to ensure safe constellation design and traffic management; if not, inter-governmental agencies will need to step up to the task.

To modify an old adage: we do not inherit Earth orbit, but borrow it from future missions!

THREE   RESPONSIBLE OPERATIONS IN SPACE

T he preceding chapters discussed the international legal framework within which national activities exist, and how states establish space policy, perform interagency coordination, and supervise and regulate their national activities through legislation, licensing, and authorization.

This chapter focuses on space activities themselves, and is divided into pre-launch, launch, on-orbit, and end-of-life issues. As a result, it is also more technological and operational in perspective than previous chapters. It gives concrete guidance to new actors in space—whether they are new states, start-up companies, or academic and university-led projects—as they begin their space activities. The best practices contained in this chapter are the types of behaviors that responsible actors will observe if they want to conduct successful space operations while also preserving order, fostering cooperation, and ensuring the long-term sustainability of space activities.

PRE-LAUNCH

Space activities begin well before a satellite is actually launched into space. In addition to designing and building the spacecraft, there are a number of policy, legal, and administrative steps that need to be taken into consideration. The following topics are deeply connected to the operational side of any space activity and should be considered well before launch and the commencement of operations in space.

Licensing
In many cases a satellite operator or other new actor needs to get one or more licenses for their space activities. These licenses include radio frequency, remote sensing, and launch vehicle operations. National governments generally administer this access through licenses that satellite operators are required to obtain before they are permitted to launch their system(s). Launch operators must also obtain licenses, which might separately pertain to launch activities and to re-entry activities.

Licensing Requirements

Licensing requirements affect most aspects of space operations, including telecommunications and remote sensing operations, launch services, and the operations of satellite ground stations on Earth (satellite Earth stations). The issuing of licenses is one of the means states use to maintain compliance with their treaty obligations, as discussed in Chapter One. Licenses cover a range of topics including spectrum access, national security oversight, compliance with insurance and safety requirements, and space debris mitigation guidelines. Satellite and launch operators are responsible for applying for and securing licenses from the relevant national regulatory authorities where they are headquartered or where they will be conducting operations. The regulatory authorities responsible for issuing licenses vary by country and domain of operations, and may include national space agencies, national telecommunications agencies, and national trade or economic agencies.

Frequency Licensing

In the satellite telecommunications segment, a primary purpose of licensing requirements is the coordination and allocation of radiofrequency spectrum on a domestic and international basis. Operators seeking to deploy a satellite communications system must apply for a license to operate that system. As spectrum is a limited resource, the licensing process acts to ensure fair access to that resource while providing a mechanism to limit the potential for interference between satellite systems, and between satellite systems and terrestrial uses of the same or adjacent radiofrequencies.

As covered in Chapter Two: Public Oversight and National Administration, regulators have generally implemented a licensing regime that ensures coordination and compliance with International Telecommunication Union (ITU) policies and regulations. In many jurisdictions, the regulator responsible for issuing a license to a communications satellite operator is the same authority responsible for making ITU submissions for that country. This is not, however, always the case; for example, in the United Kingdom (UK), the Office of Communications (Ofcom) is responsible for ITU filings while the UK Space Agency is the licensing authority.

In general, any operator seeking to operate a satellite system that will receive or transmit data (including command and control linkages) over the radiofrequency spectrum must apply for a license from its relevant regulatory agency. Prospective operators must provide a range of technical and business information to the regulator when submitting license applications. In general, license applications must contain technical data describing the system including the spectral bands to be used, a planned implementation timeline, and information concerning financial ability to construct, launch, and operate the system. Applications may also require detail on the steps to be taken to reduce interference potential through coordination with other operators, as well as a post-mission disposal plan that takes into account space debris mitigation guidelines.

Some regulators also require operators to obtain licenses for the ground stations used to communicate with the satellites, including end-user terminal equipment (traditionally referred to as "Earth stations"). Earth station licenses serve to reduce the potential for radiofrequency interference, in particular interference with other terrestrial applications, and may also include provisions to evaluate physical interference with other applications, such as aviation. Earth station license applications typically require similar technical and business details to satellite network applications. For end-user terminals, the licensing authority may issue blanket licenses covering technically identical equipment.

Remote Sensing Licenses

In compliance with the international regime discussed in Chapter One and also discussed in the in-depth analysis on Remote Sensing at the end of Chapter Two, national governments may also require commercial remote sensing satellite operators to apply for a license covering the imaging capabilities of the satellite system. These licenses may be issued by authorities separate from those responsible for the communications systems aspects. Remote sensing licenses are typically required to ensure coordination with national security policies. Required information to be submitted may include system technical details; expected dates of operation; launch information; data acquisition, access, and distribution plans; data pricing policy; planned agreements with foreign entities; and a post-mission disposal plan. Remote sensing licenses may apply conditions on the operator, such as resolution restrictions and the ability to restrict imaging of national territory.

Launch and Re-Entry Licenses

Entities providing commercial launch services are typically required to obtain a launch license from a national authority, which may differ from the authority responsible for other space-related licenses. Launch licenses may be specific to launch operations or re-entry operations, and may have varying requirements based on whether the launch (or re-entry) vehicle is experimental or operational, and whether it is expendable or reusable.

Launch and re-entry licenses authorize an operator to conduct one or more launches or re-entries defined by a specific set of operational parameters, which are codified in (and authorized by) the license. These parameters generally include, but are not limited to: mission names, intended launch windows and trajectory, parameters for the payload(s) intended and final orbits, ground and flight safety plans, accident investigation plans, and re-entry windows and trajectory (if applicable). Typically, operators are also required to submit information demonstrating that their intended launch operations are in compliance with environmental policies, export control regulations, other licensing requirements (e.g., frequency and remote sensing), and insurance and liability coverage obligations.

In order to obtain a license, the launch providers may request information from the operators of the satellites to be launched. The process of obtaining a launch license entails multiple steps and submissions to the regulatory authority. Accordingly, the authorities often offer pre-application consultation services so that operators are aware of the steps and information required before they initiate the process.

Launch and re-entry licenses serve numerous purposes. They act to protect public safety interests including protection of third-party safety on the ground and coordination with air traffic management functions. The licensing process provides national authorities with the ability to review the intended launch operation against national security considerations and other national regulations and requirements. The launch licensing process also acts to ensure that national authorities collect the information necessary to satisfy international registration requirements for the launch.

The Licensing Process: Getting a License

The licensing process imposes obligations on both the government agencies issuing the licenses and the operators who are the licensees. The license approval process typically includes an inter-agency coordination process in which the licensing authority consults with other government agencies who might be affected by, or have oversight of, the proposed operation. This reduces the administrative burden on the operator by reducing the number of consultations they must undertake. Licensing authorities also may have an obligation to conduct technical and financial due diligence on applications received. This helps reduce the number of frivolous applications received, and helps prevent resources (such as spectrum) from being allocated to operators who are unable to use it. Operators should be prepared to respond to due-diligence requests during the license approval process.

When applying for a license, operators should be aware of potential administrative fees and the time required to process the application. Fees are intended to allow the issuing authority to recover costs associated with processing the applications. Application processing times vary, but can be significant depending upon the efficiency of the authority and the amount of interagency coordination required. For applications requiring full coordination and processing with the ITU, the processing time required can be measured in years. System deployment plans must account for these processing times.

Licensing applications, processes, and requirements may differ by operating domain or type of system. Systems operating in geostationary Earth orbit (GEO) may be subject to a different process than those operating in other orbits. In the telecommunications segment, Fixed Satellite Services (FSS), Mobile Satellite Services (MSS), and Broadcasting Satellite Services (BSS) can have differing licensing processes. Some national regulators may offer less onerous licensing requirements for amateur satellite operators, and some authorities responsible for launch operations offer distinctions between experimental and operational systems. It is the responsibility of the operator to ascertain which categories are applicable to their system, although national authorities may offer consultation on this subject. During the application process, applicants should also be aware that some national regulators make applications public (either in total or in part) and may also allow public commentary on applications. This may present implications for business strategy.

Once a license is issued, the operator is responsible for various continuing reporting requirements. Licenses typically have a validity period, after which a renewal application may be required. Satellite operators are commonly required to report any major changes in system operations or performance, including technical faults, to the licensing authority, and may also be required to submit annual performance reports. These reporting requirements satisfy the licensing authority's obligation to provide continuing oversight of licensees.

Launch Vehicle Selection

When selecting a launch vehicle, satellite operators, especially new operators, usually hire a technical consultant to advise on launch vehicle selection. The technical consultant is usually an experienced industry veteran knowledgeable about the range of considerations involved. The satellite operator and technical consultant then request technical assessments from launch operators to determine whether a launch vehicle is capable of accommodating the operator's specific satellite mission. A group of qualified launch operators are asked to submit a proposal. Launch proposals are evaluated by the satellite operator and technical consultants.

If a satellite operator requires launch insurance (and most operators do require insurance in order to meet financial obligations and licensing requirements), an insurance broker will likely work with the satellite operator and the proposed launch providers to determine the appropriate insurance rates. If possible, it is important for a satellite operator to work closely with a launch provider and to have an independent representative on-site and participating in a launch provider's operations. Insurance is discussed later in this chapter. It is important to select a launch vehicle with adequate performance capability and appropriate performance margin to accommodate modest satellite mass growth if necessary. Launch service providers will not allow their limits to be exceeded because this will result in catastrophic failure or deployment into an incorrect orbit.

Launch providers normally have a queue of payloads waiting to be launched. Conducting a space launch is a complex endeavor requiring coordination of many complicated tasks that are affected by a variety of factors that are difficult to control. The launch vehicle and satellites are often composed of components manufactured by dozens to hundreds of suppliers. Those components must be tested to ensure proper function before and during integration between the satellite and the launch vehicle. Any anomalies discovered during testing often require disassembly and further testing. Furthermore, failure of a satellite or launch vehicle in orbit that shares hardware with a new satellite in manufacture may require a delay in production until the cause of the other mission's failure is determined. Even if a spacecraft and launch vehicle show up at the launch site on schedule, it may be necessary to wait for the launches of other payloads that have priority but have experienced schedule slips. Once on the launch pad, weather and launch-range issues can further delay a launch. All of these factors lead to the reality that many launches do not occur when originally scheduled.

A new satellite operator must be financially prepared to survive a significant launch delay which could require expensive satellite storage fees and a lack of planned revenue from satellite operations.

A new satellite operator must be financially prepared to survive a significant launch delay which could require expensive satellite storage fees and a lack of planned revenue from satellite operations.

Integrating Multiple Payloads

There are multiple ways a launch provider can integrate multiple payloads into the same launch. One of the most proven forms of multi-payload launch deployment is satellite stacking. The Russian *Proton* heavy-launch vehicle stacks two satellites, with the lower satellite carrying the mass of the upper satellite through an appropriate interface. Alternatively, the European *Ariane-5* launch vehicle uses a rigid structure, a type of shelf that carries the mass of the upper satellite, instead of it resting on the lower satellite.

Some satellites are designed from the beginning to be launched together in an efficient, clustered manner. The French-Italian satellite manufacturer Thales Alenia Space designs spacecraft buses, such as those used in the Iridium constellation, to be efficiently clustered to take advantage of lower cost launch options. Designing for clustering from the start is particularly common with large constellations of smaller satellites, several of which can be launched into the same orbital plane at the same time. For example, the Iridium low Earth orbit (LEO) communications constellation was designed to have 66 operational satellites spread across 11 orbital planes. Except for the occasional solo launch, most of the Iridium satellites were launched in groups of four and six on American, Russian, and Chinese launch vehicles.

For other satellite missions, it is more efficient to deploy a payload into space on another operator's satellite, a technique known as a hosted payload, thereby negating the need to build and launch a dedicated satellite. In a hosted payload configuration, the payload owner pays the host spacecraft operator to carry an instrument that uses the host satellite's utilities, such as power, data transfer, etc. Finally, as new, large constellations of communications satellites have been announced, a concept called a hosted bus has emerged. In this configuration, a satellite operator can purchase a spacecraft based on the same bus as the other satellites in the constellation. The hosted bus operator benefits because the non-recurring engineering costs of the satellite bus have been paid for by the constellation operator, making the hosted bus satellite much less expensive to build. Another major benefit is that the hosted bus operator can use the constellation's communications network and ground infrastructure, and may be able to ride-share a launch for a relatively low price.

More recently, the concept of launching multiple payloads from multiple operators on the same launch, known as a rideshare, has become popular. A rideshare, at its most basic level, can be defined as multiple satellites sharing the same launch vehicle. Many satellite operators, especially those operating small satellites or cubesats, may elect to launch as a secondary payload rather than as a primary purchaser of a launch vehicle. As a secondary payload, operators are taking advantage of surplus payload volume and mass margin to essentially share a ride on a launch purchased by another satellite operator. Entities wishing to pursue launch in a ridesharing arrangement might contract directly with a launch operator or with a satellite operator. They might also work through a launch broker service, which matches payloads to launch opportunities. Some launch brokers may themselves purchase a dedicated launch opportunity and aggregate multiple payloads together.

Ridesharing arrangements are typically lower in cost than purchasing a dedicated launch, which may be cost-prohibitive for many new actors. However, the approach has its drawbacks. Secondary payloads typically have a reduced ability to influence the schedule of the launch, which is usually negotiated between the launch operator and the primary payload operator. Secondary payloads may also find themselves with limited orbital insertion options and facing a suboptimal vibration and acoustic environment during launch, as these parameters are defined according to the mission requirements of the primary payload. Furthermore, a rideshare increases the complexity of the launch and deployment and therefore increases the risk of failure. A variety of rideshare hazards must be assessed prior to launch, including explosive hazards, electromagnetic compatibility, electrical shock, battery rupture, electrolyte leakage, sharp edges, protrusions, and premature mechanism deployment.

Launch Services Agreement

Securing a launch to outer space with a launch provider will require entering into a legally binding contract called a launch services agreement. The launch services agreement will methodically define all the particulars of launching, and give definitions for many elements of the launch. The agreement delineates all the particular roles and responsibilities of the actors, but in general, these are that the customer will be handing over a satellite that is fit for launch, and the launch provider will be performing certain services, such as successfully integrating the satellite into the rocket and safely and successfully launching it into the correct orbit.

Each launch services agreement will include unique elements for each particular launch, but—as with most contracts—it will always have certain elements that make it sufficient as a legally binding contract. While the contracts that companies use may seem lengthy, deal in minutiae, and address scenarios that might not happen (such as launch failures and other mishaps), legal contracts are actually nuanced documents in that they refine all of the various shared understandings and expectations of the parties into a finite number of words that address all details, define all roles, assign risks, and do so in a fashion that would stand up in court as being a valid contract. A contract is a written reflection of the parties' shared understanding of what they undertake to do.

So that both the launch provider and the customer have the exact same understanding of particular words, a launch contract will define its most important terms. The definitions section of a contract might define the following: "satellite," "launch services," "launch opportunity," "launch vehicle," "launch window," "launch" or "launching," "post-launches services," "shared launch," "third party," "auxiliary payload," "launch abort," "launch failure," "partial failure," and other important terms. Because they are defined, each party is held to understand these terms, and to agree to them upon entering into the contract.

The implications of this should be clear. For example, "launch failure" might be defined differently than "partial launch failure," and should the unfortunate occur and the satellite not be placed into the correct orbit, the resulting situation might be categorized as a launch failure—or perhaps only a partial launch failure. This categorization might have a direct impact on the triggering of insurance and even liability provisions. The definitions in the launch contract matter, and should be deeply scrutinized by the parties.

Another component of the launch services agreement are the sections listing the undertakings to be executed by both sides. Sometimes called the commitments, or technical commitments, these enumerate precisely what each side must do so that the other side can fulfill its obligations under the contract. Because launching advanced hardware to outer space is such a technological achievement, the parties are essentially becoming partners with each other for a certain amount of time.

Last, parties to a launch contract must face the possibility of disaster, and consider, negotiate, and agree upon what risks are borne by whom, what rights are accorded in the case of certain events, and what roles each party must play. A section of the contract will contain some allocation of potential liabilities and risks.

Standard contracts outside of the space industry have a clause sometimes called a *force majeure* clause, which means that an intervening, supervening, or otherwise unpredictable "act of God" will excuse the parties from undertaking their commitments under the contract.

Insurance

Insurance may be required by the national regulatory authority licensing and supervising the space activities. It might also be required by the launch services provider in the launch services agreement. A launch buyer may procure insurance to minimize exposure resulting from a launch failure. Generally, launch vehicles with a less reliable track record have more expensive insurance while more reliable systems have less expensive insurance. Therefore, insurance can balance out the price differential between low-price, high-risk launch options and high-price, more reliable launch providers. The most commonly purchased insurance is launch insurance, which extends coverage from launch-vehicle ignition to in-orbit delivery. A separate policy, if required, is purchased to cover satellite failure during its operational phase in orbit. A launch buyer should also be aware of the liability environments in the nations hosting the launch providers. If a launch failure causes damage to the uninvolved public, a buyer may be exposed to liability. Some nations have put in place indemnification regimes that establish a maximum third-party liability level so that damages in excess of that amount are paid for by the national government.

Pre-Launch Payload Testing

Launching a satellite into space exposes it to significant vibration and acoustic forces, shock, coupled loads, and thermal and electromagnetic effects. Satellite designers and engineers need to reference a launch vehicle's user guide for information about the environment during launch, and properly test a spacecraft to make sure it will survive the launch. These risks may also extend into the early phases of a satellite's on-orbit activities, particularly if it will be undergoing weeks of maneuvering to reach its final orbit. Steps can be taken during the design, engineering, and testing phases of satellite development to prepare a spacecraft for successful deployment.

During the design phase, it may be advisable to select a satellite bus—the main body of the satellite—that has significant legacy space experience. Commonly used satellite designs should have significant data collected about how the spacecraft structure and components handle a launch environment. Furthermore, using a proven satellite and launch-vehicle combination further reduces the risk of payload deployment failures.

Spacecraft must be designed to handle the vibration and acoustic effects generated by rocket motors as a satellite is launched into space. A spacecraft will be exposed to at least three types of vibro-acoustic environments that occur during launch, including random vibration, sine vibration, and acoustically induced vibration. The greatest vibro-acoustic effects are present during the first minutes of a launch, as overpressure and reverberations are the strongest. This is followed by flow noise as air streams over the payload fairing, causing reverberating sound within, and is particularly strong during flight through high-dynamic pressure, such as transition through the sound barrier. Information about the vibro-acoustic environment of a launch system can be found in a launch vehicle's user guide.

Most ground testing regimes simplify the launch environment and test to the most extreme conditions, not the specific mission profile. Therefore, if a spacecraft design is susceptible to vibrational effects, a non-standard, more spacecraft-specific vibration testing regime should be developed. Vibration effects can be mitigated during the design and engineering phases by incorporating motion control solutions to aid in attenuating sine vibration events and random vibration created by the launch vehicle.

Spacecraft will experience short, intense transient accelerations with broad frequency content and a very short duration, generally less than 20 milliseconds. These shocks occur during specific flight actions, such as the severing of a spent stage with an explosive charge, and can be straightforwardly modeled and tested on the ground. The hazards of shock can be mitigated by using non-pyrotechnic bolt-cutter-type release mechanisms.

In addition to taking account of the effects of vibro-acoustics and shock generated by a launch vehicle, it is also necessary to understand the coupled loads generated by the interaction of a launch vehicle and spacecraft as a complete structural system. There are a variety of methods to model coupled loads, but their quality and accuracy are highly dependent on the spacecraft's structural dynamic model and data gathered from flights. During the course of a satellite's design and launch-vehicle selection process, it is wise to iteratively update a coupled load's model as the spacecraft design matures and more data about the force environment of a launch system are collected.

During the launch and orbit raising phase, the thermal environment has to be maintained within the bounds for which the electronics and deployment mechanisms have been designed and qualified. Different methods are used to ensure this. At the launch pad, the capsule of the launch vehicle is air-conditioned or heated to maintain the limits of the temperature excursion. After the fairing is deployed, the launch vehicle rotates to expose the satellite to the sun to keep the temperature inside of the satellite within the allowable temperature range acceptable to the electronics, and to warm the deployment mechanisms.

During launch, spacecraft will be exposed to various electromagnetic environments, including energy from tracking radars, launch vehicle radiofrequency (RF) transmitters, flight through regions of energetic protons, and atmospheric lightning. Therefore, during the engineering phase, it is important to strictly adhere to electromagnetic design specifications, and to model possible occurrences of electrical interference. System-level compatibility between a spacecraft and launch vehicle is addressed through integrated avionics testing during manufacturing, with attention to bonding and isolation requirements for a launch vehicle. Full system integration testing occurs at the launch site.

The Links Between Testing and Anomaly Mitigation

The importance of the design, manufacturing, and testing of a spacecraft cannot be overemphasized when it comes to mitigating on-orbit anomalies. For all but human missions, these phases present the only opportunity for true "hands-on" and re-engineering time with the system. The following list provides best practices to consider in developing a process from the pre-operational phase to the phases for reducing occurrences of, and impact from, certain on-orbit anomalies:

- ☑ Perform a detailed Failure Modes and Effects Analysis (FMEA) at multiple phases of design and eliminate single-point failures wherever possible.
- ☑ Leverage FMEA results to develop robust and detailed operational procedures and execute these during the integration and test (I&T) phase to characterize system behavior with an opportunity to update prior to launch.
- ☑ Catalog and save all documentation and test data including vendor-provided material. This information can be critical to determining the root cause of an on-orbit failure.
- ☑ Develop a flight-like simulator and/or engineering model of the system. A robust simulator is an invaluable tool for testing complex operational procedures, validating firmware and software upgrades, and performing detailed root cause investigations.
- ☑ Ensure the design of the spacecraft provides ample data for diagnosing anomalies by incorporating sufficient telemetry access points providing insight from every unit onboard a vehicle and developing detailed and well-organized telemetry formats.

Practices such as these help the satellite operator understand the risk inherent in the mission profile (space environment and operations requirements) and design to mitigate those risks.

Launch Mission Assurance

Launch operations deploying satellites rely on a partnership between the launch operator and the launch buyer to implement a process and culture focused on mission success. This type of relationship and process, called mission assurance, is a standard that is perhaps not feasible for smaller commercial budgets, but can be employed by large-scale buyers, such as national governments. Mission assurance as a process is an iterative and continuous technical and management activity employed over the entire lifecycle of a launch system. To achieve success, the mission assurance process must include a disciplined application of systems engineering, risk management, quality assurance, and program management principles.

Key features of mission assurance include a launch procurement strategy that includes adequate contingency funding, which then ensures that the launch provider maintains the workforce, facilities, and data-sharing required to perform integration and launch, handle contingencies, and reach agreement when issues arise. Another key feature of mission assurance is clear accountability, which requires that a single entity is responsible for understanding, tracking, and ensuring that flight worthiness is maintained.

Next, continuity and independent verification require that funding is available to maintain the depth of independent technical capabilities to analyze potential issues and render assessment of spaceflight worthiness. Finally, it is necessary to conduct extensive reviews; both those leading to the spaceflight worthiness certification and the go/no-go decision for launch, as well as post-flight data reviews.

LAUNCH

Launching an object into orbit requires a huge amount of energy. At present, that energy is created using immensely energetic chemical reactions taking place in extremely complicated machines that often are attached to very expensive payloads. Significant care must be taken to both increase the odds of a successful space launch and minimize the risk that space launch activities pose to people, ground installations, and air and maritime vehicles. The launch phase is considered the most dangerous time period during any space project.

There have been satellite launches from approximately 30 sites around the world. Today, most launches occur from roughly a dozen launch facilities. Creating and safely operating a launch facility requires thorough consideration of launch safety, environmental, and ground safety issues. Spaceports are generally located in sparsely populated regions to minimize the risk that a launch failure could harm people or property in the area. Spaceports are also often located near oceans or deserts so that a rocket's ascent trajectory overflies large, relatively uninhabited regions in order to minimize public exposure to expelled rocket stages or other falling debris. Once a site for a launch facility is identified, a national government often requires completion of an environmental assessment to ensure that operation of a launch facility will not pollute or disrupt natural wildlife habitat to an unreasonable extent. Finally, the design and operations of a spaceport need to follow best practices that have evolved at established spaceports.

There are no globally agreed-upon rules for how to develop and operate a space launch facility. Spaceports are usually developed as national assets and are managed by government agencies. Many states have conducted studies to determine a path forward toward commercial spaceport development. Some states have taken steps to incentivize and enable development of commercially operated spaceports. The US has created the most proactive commercial spaceport regulatory regime thus far, and other states often reference US regulations.

Terrestrial Environmental Safety Considerations

The terrestrial environmental impact of constructing and operating a proposed launch site may be significant, and the relevant national authority will likely require an environmental impact analysis. Developers of launch facilities need to take into account the effect of launch activities on various environmental domains including the atmosphere, noise sources and effects, and surface environments.

One environmental concern is the impact space launches have on the atmosphere. Ambient air near Earth's surface is often regulated by national air-quality standards to ensure pollutant levels do not reach damaging levels. Due to their ultra-hazardous effect on ambient air quality if they are accidentally released, the storage and use of some high-energy and volatile rocket fuels may be of unique concern. In addition, some launch vehicles emit hazardous gases even during normal operation. Other types of launch vehicles, especially those with solid rocket motors, emit various type of particles when traveling through the upper layers of atmosphere, which may come under increased scrutiny by environmental regulators in the future.

A second major source of environmental concern is noise. The amount of noise created by a proposed launch facility needs be understood and evaluated in the context of the natural noise environment. Rocket launches tend to generate significant amounts of noise that can disrupt wildlife habitats. Sonic booms generated by launch and re-entry activities along a trajectory may cause further damage to wildlife, property, and human physiology.

Finally, launch facilities are often placed in areas that are remote from human populations, but may also be pristine wildlife habitats. Land, marine, wetland, and other surface environments surrounding a launch site may each have unique features requiring protection. Site-specific studies and impact mitigation plans should be in place prior to construction. Developing a launch facility near areas containing threatened and endangered species habitats should be especially avoided.

The tensions among spaceport activity, wildlife habitat, and economic interests were demonstrated in Japan's decisions around the amount of launch activity allowed at the Tanegashima Space Center in southern Japan. Launch activity was initially limited to a 190-day annual window with a cap of 17 total launches per year in order to address local concerns that launch activity could negatively impact the fishing industry. After further study of the environmental impact and a recognition of the need to launch year-round to be commercially competitive, Japan lifted the restrictions in 2011. In Europe, the European Union's Registration, Evaluation, Authorisation and Restriction of Chemicals (EU REACH) regulation applies to all EU entities, including the aerospace sector, and might be investigated by actors looking to conduct activities there.

Ground Safety Considerations

Once appropriate environmental concerns are addressed, a national regulatory entity will likely require a policy review to ensure that a proposed new space launch facility would not jeopardize national security, foreign-policy interests, or international obligations of the hosting nation.

Next, casualty risk assessment will be conducted. Launch sites should be placed in areas where launch activities will not jeopardize public health and safety or the safety of property. Therefore, the flight corridor for a launch vehicle—the land under its launch trajectory—must be adequately unpopulated so that there is a minimum chance of damages should the rocket vehicle or spent stages impact the area. Models exist to calculate the risk to the public, and some nations, such as the United States, set minimum quantitative casualty risk levels.

Because of the explosive nature of many solid and liquid propellants, another key part of the initial design of a space launch facility is the creation of an explosives site plan that shows the location of all explosive hazard facilities, the distances between them, and the distances to public areas. Safe handling and management of explosive launch-vehicle propellants is critical. Standards exist to guide construction of launch site infrastructure in order to avoid causes of accidental explosions, such as lightning, static electricity, electric supply system problems and electromagnetic radiation.

To ensure safe space launch facility operations, it is important for an operator to address controlling public access, scheduling operations at the site, notifications, recordkeeping, and launch site accident response and investigation. Access to the site should be controlled using security guards, fences, and other barriers. People entering the site should be taught the safety and emergency response procedures. Alarms and other warning signals are necessary for informing people at the site of an emergency situation. If a launch site has multiple users on the site at the same time, the site operator should have procedures for scheduling operations so that the activities of one do not create hazards for the other.

Hazard areas are another particular concern. Coordination with the national maritime and air traffic control entities is necessary to limit how closely aircraft and watercraft can approach launch and re-entry operational hazard areas. Notices to Mariners are issued for spaceports near waterways when launch activities are being conducted. The notices require vessels to clear hazard areas during specific windows of time. Alternatively, Notices to Airmen (NOTAMs) are issued for areas surrounding a launch facility and beneath a launch corridor when expected casualty calculations exceed specified thresholds. When a launch facility conducts a flight operation, the appropriate equipment to track a launch vehicle's progress across the launch range must be aboard the launch vehicle and on the ground.

Range Safety During Launch Operations

The launch of a satellite requires significant planning, coordination, and risk management. Range safety operations have evolved over time at launch facilities around the globe. Standards that are in development by the International Organization for Standardization (ISO) identify safe practices that apply to launch site operations, flight safety systems, and other areas. Globally, most spaceports are operated by national governments and have varying approaches to the specific range safety practices. However, core principles are common. Range safety practices discussed in this section most often reference the commercial regulations developed and implemented by the US Federal Aviation Administration (FAA).

First, a flight safety analysis is conducted by a launch operator for each launch in order to control the risk to the public from hazards created during both a normal and a malfunctioning launch-vehicle flight. A risk assessment analysis should account for the variability associated with each source of hazard during flight, the normal flight and each failure response mode of the launch vehicle, and each external and launch-vehicle flight environment. Additionally, a risk assessment should consider populations potentially exposed to the flight, and the performance of any flight safety system (including time delays associated with the systems).

The outputs of a risk assessment are used to create a plan to sufficiently isolate the hazard to keep risk to the public within acceptable quantitative limits. A summary of the various analyses required as part of a flight safety analysis are identified in Table 6.

Flight Safety Analyses	
Trajectory	Toxic release hazard
Overflight gate	Flight safety limits
Probability of failure	Time-delay
Malfunction turn	Far-field overpressure blast effects
Hold-and-resume gate	Straight-up time
Ground debris risk	Flight hazard-area
Orbital debris	Collision avoidance
Data loss flight time and planned safe flight state	

Table 6 – Flight Safety Analyses

Public Risk Criteria

National regulatory entities such as the US FAA set specific quantitative criteria for the risk exposure of the public that launch operations must meet. These standards consist of specific probabilities of risk to the public from inert and explosive debris, toxic release, and far-field blast overpressure. These quantitative limits do not apply to aircraft or watercraft, and as a result, a launch operator must establish hazard areas with rules requiring the removal of waterborne vessels and aircraft from the hazard zone during the launch activity.

Flight Termination System

In order to meet public risk criteria, it is necessary to incorporate self-destruct systems on launch vehicles. Activation of a destruct system breaks the launch vehicle into smaller debris, burns off fuel, and keeps overpressure effects isolated from the public. Termination criteria are developed during various flight safety analyses and implemented as part of the written flight safety plan. Flight termination systems are a critical element of range safety. There are some exceptions to this rule, especially in the older rocket systems that use toxic fuels, in which case it is preferable for the rocket to destruct farther from the launch site on a trajectory that is routed into non-populated areas.

Flight Safety Plan

Based on the conclusions reached during the flight safety analysis, a written flight safety plan defines how launch processing and flight of a launch vehicle will be conducted without adversely affecting public safety and how to respond to a launch mishap. A flight safety plan should identify the flight safety personnel who will approve and implement each part of the plan.

Elements of a flight safety plan include flight safety rules, a flight safety system, data on trajectory, and debris dispersion data. The plan must also identify flight hazard areas that must be cleared and controlled during launch, and support systems and services including any aircraft or ship that a launch operator will use. Last, the plan must have a description of the flight safety-related tests, reviews, rehearsals, and other safety operations.

A ground safety plan describes the implementation of hazard controls that have been identified by a launch operator's ground safety analysis and that address all public-safety-related issues. The plan should at least include a description of the launch vehicle and any payload (or class of payload), and identify each hazard, including explosives, propellants, toxics and other hazardous materials, radiation sources, and pressurized systems. The plan must also include figures that show the location of each hazard on the launch vehicle and indicate where at the launch site a launch operator performs hazardous operations during launch processing.

A variety of other plans are necessary as part of a flight safety plan, including:

- Launch support equipment and instrumentation plan
- Local agreements and public coordination plans
- Frequency management plan
- Hazard-area surveillance and clearance plan
- Flight termination system electronic piece-parts program plan
- Communications plan
- Accident investigation plan
- Countdown plan

Safety-Critical Preflight Operations

A launch operator must perform safety-critical preflight operations that protect the public from the adverse effects of hazards associated with launch processing and the flight of a launch vehicle. For example, a launch countdown plan should be distributed to all personnel responsible for the countdown and flight of a launch vehicle. Any nearby region of land, sea, or air necessary to the launch should be assessed and monitored to ensure the number and locations of members of the public meet established safety standards. The operator should monitor the weather to identify meteorological conditions that could threaten the safe performance of a launch, such as the presence of lightning. To ensure accuracy, data verification of launch-vehicle tracking should be employed.

If the launch vehicle exits flight boundaries, the readiness of flight safety systems must be ensured if intentional destruction of the launch vehicle is required. At least two tracking sources should be available prior to lift-off, and no less than one verified tracking source at all times from lift-off to orbit insertion for an orbital launch, or to the end of powered flight for a suborbital launch.

ON-ORBIT ACTIVITIES

Each day, more than 1,500 operational satellites orbit the Earth performing a variety of missions critical to the global economy and security. Remotely operating these spacecraft to ensure mission assurance and safety of flight requires managing a variety of risks—not the least of which is avoiding running into other active satellites and the hundreds of thousands of pieces of space debris also orbiting the Earth. The following sections provide a more detailed discussion of the major issues that satellite operators need to deal with in order to ensure the well-being of their satellites and prevent collisions or incidents that could undermine the long-term sustainability of the space environment.

Satellite Orbit Determination and Tracking

The first step is for satellite operators to be able to know where their own satellite is in orbit, and know the locations of other objects that may pose a collision risk. Unlike our having the ability to find our position on Earth using a global positioning system (GPS), the majority of satellites in Earth orbit currently do not or cannot use GPS. And neither do any of the hundreds of thousands of pieces of debris. As such, the vast majority of space objects must be observed using systems which do not rely on the cooperation of the object being tracked in order to determine their orbit. Traditionally this is known as space surveillance, or more recently as space situational awareness (SSA).

Satellite operators need to determine how they will obtain orbital trajectory information on their satellites and other space objects. Satellite orbit determination (OD) is the process by which operators or third parties can obtain knowledge of the satellite's trajectory, usually relative to the center of mass of Earth. The basic theory involves determining a satellite's position and velocity—its state—at a specific time in the past, and then using a set of differential equations that model changes in its position and velocity over time to predict where it will be in the future. In aerospace terms, this is "generating an ephemeris," which is a set of points in space that define the future trajectory of a satellite. A significant challenge in performing accurate OD is developing precise and accurate equations of motion that include the various natural forces or perturbations that act on the satellite, such as irregularities in Earth's gravity, atmospheric drag, and the gravitational pull of the sun and the moon.

Satellite OD begins with data on the position and velocity of a satellite, known as observations. A single observation measures a satellite's position, and perhaps velocity as well, at a specific moment in time, and relative to the location of a specific sensor. Multiple observations taken over a single period of time are called a track. The observations from one sensor can be used by themselves or combined with data from other sensors which observe the space object at other points in its orbit.

Different measurement types have different characteristics, and these lead to different levels of confidence in satellite state elements estimated from these measurements. Traditionally, the main source of data has been collected by ground-based radars and ground-based and space-based telescopes. Telescopes may also use satellite laser ranging (SLR) techniques to directly illuminate satellites using a laser source, rather than relying on illumination from the sun. Radar observations can provide velocity information and typically have excellent angular tracking, but can suffer from poor range rate estimations. SLR can derive excellent range and range rate estimations while having poor estimations of angular rates.

No matter the type of sensor, it is important to understand the accuracy and precision of the tracking data it provides. Often, sensors are periodically tasked with tracking calibration spheres or other space objects whose orbit is well-known in order to determine their accuracy. If a sensor's measurements are consistently off true, a deliberate bias can be introduced to correct some or all of the error. The historical performance of sensors can be tracked in order to determine their accuracy and precision over time, which in turn can be used as a weighting factor for valuing their data relative to other sensors.

Accurately tracking a space object requires collecting observations from many parts of its orbit. That means a global network of sensors is required, which can be terrestrial or space-based. To operate and maintain such a network has historically been expensive, and as a result, tracking satellites and space debris has been primarily a governmental function. To date, the US government has been the primary source of this type of information to the public, via the US military's Joint Space Operations Center (JSpOC), although there are increasingly other sources of tracking information (both governmental and non-governmental) available to satellite operators.

Orbit Propagation

Knowing where an object is now, however, is only part of the problem, since there is also a need to know where an object will be in the future to assess the risk of collision. That means understanding the various forces acting on an orbital object—Earth gravity, solar and lunar gravitational effects, solar radiation pressure, and atmospheric drag, the last of which presents a major challenge for LEO objects. Much scientific research has gone into developing mathematical models to estimate how these and other natural forces—known as perturbations—affect satellite trajectories over time. But one force can be extremely difficult to model: the thrust used to maneuver a spacecraft. Most active spacecraft have to maneuver periodically to maintain the orbit needed to perform their mission. A maneuver that takes place during the timeframe of a future prediction—such as the probability of whether the satellite will collide with another object—will invalidate the analysis. Thus, accurate modeling and predictions need to take into account both models of natural perturbations and any planned maneuvers.

The good news is that the satellite operator must know this information well in order to perform their mission. Sharing the information with other operators can provide more timely updates and avoid confusion as a result of not knowing an operator's intentions. The challenge is that each operator typically uses their own coordinate systems (and sometimes different time systems), which means they all have to be normalized—or put in a common reference system—to be useful. This process requires a full understanding of units, coordinate and time definitions, and a way to validate that information, since many satellite systems were not designed to interoperate with those of other operators, only to be internally consistent.

The results also need to be shared in a standard way to ensure that each operator knows how to understand and apply that normalized data. And that sharing needs to be done on a regular basis to ensure a common understanding of how to apply the data and to avoid the possibility of misinterpretation in the midst of responding to a serious event.

Two Techniques for Combining Observations into a State

Two main techniques are used for combining multiple observations into a single state for a satellite. The traditional technique is known as the batch processor, and it is based on the well-known method of least squares mathematical technique, which selects the final solution that minimizes the distance between all of the observed locations of a space object and the projected trajectory.

While the simplest version of the batch least squares technique is relatively straightforward and easy to calculate, it has three major shortcomings. The first is that each observation error is weighted equally even though the accuracy of the observations may differ widely. An inaccurate observation from one sensor is given just as much weight in the final estimate as a very accurate observation from a different sensor. The second major problem is that the observations may be correlated with each other, and using correlated observations in a simple least squares solution violates one of its underlying mathematical assumptions. Third, the batch least squares method does not consider that the errors are samples from a random process and makes no attempt to utilize any statistical information.

To overcome these limitations, a method of determining a weighted least squares solution and the minimum variance is implemented. The weighted least squares solution selects an estimate x as the value that minimizes the weighted sum of the squares of the calculated observation errors. This algorithm for determining a state estimate is referred to as the "batch processor." The name derives from the fact that all data generally are accumulated beforehand and processed in a single batch to determine the solution. The batch formulation provides an estimate of the state at some chosen epoch or time period using an entire batch of data. This estimate and its associated covariance matrix can then be mapped to other times.

A second and more modern technique for combining multiple observations into a single state estimation is the sequential estimation algorithm. In sequential estimation, the observations are processed as soon as they are received. The sequential estimation algorithm is often referred to as the Kalman filter, and it utilizes new observations to continually correct its estimate of the future state. The sequential estimation algorithm takes an estimated state and a covariance matrix for that state and propagates them forward in time. New observations of the future state are used to recursively correct the original state. The sequential processor provides an estimate of the state at each observation time based on observations up to that time. The solution and the covariance matrix can also be mapped to other times.

Both techniques can misrepresent the actual error in the predicted state. With the sequential estimation algorithm, the state estimation error covariance matrix may approach zero as the number of observations becomes large. The magnitude of the covariance matrix elements will decrease depending on the density, information content, and accuracy of the observations. A similar effect may be seen with the batch processor, where the state estimation error covariance matrix generally underestimates the actual error in the predicted state.

Conjunction Assessment Procedures and Standards

For a satellite operator, one of the key tools for reducing on-orbit risk is to perform conjunction assessment (CA)—that is, to determine which objects might have a chance of coming close to, and possibly colliding, with your spacecraft. Conceptually, the CA task is straightforward. The operator simply needs to know where all the objects that might present a collision risk are, and be able to predict where they will be for a period far enough into the future to enable an effective course of action should a close approach be deemed unsafe. With that information, the process of screening each of the operator's satellites can be performed quickly using well-known analytical techniques. The challenge comes from understanding current limitations to performing effective CA and identifying areas for improvement.

Typically, CA is performed for a pair of trajectories, each representing the location of a space object over time, where the relative separation distance between two objects is computed over a given prediction time span. The trajectories may be generated using high-accuracy catalog data from a data-provider, or using positional data generated by the spacecraft itself. A conjunction event is where the relative separation reaches a local minimum, commonly referred to as the point of closest approach.

Operational collision risk management starts with the generation of close approach predictions and ends with an action/no-action decision from mission stakeholders. The step-by-step process consists of:

- Screening a defined set of space objects against another set of objects to identify close approaches, referred to as conjunction events;
- Reporting all conjunction events that are predicted to violate a specific separation-distance threshold over some future time span;
- Assessing and quantifying the collision threat for each conjunction event that is identified; and
- Developing and executing collision avoidance maneuvers for conjunction events that exceed the operator's risk threshold.

Potential collisions can be identified by individual spacecraft operators, operational support organizations such as Aerospace Corporation or the Space Data Association (SDA), and government organizations such as US Strategic Command (USSTRATCOM) or national space agencies. To be most useful to satellite operators, the entity conducting the conjunction analysis should have accurate trajectory data on both active satellites, including planned maneuvers within the prediction time, and other space objects.

Operational Conjunction Assessment

The conjunction assessment process occurs throughout the lifetime of a satellite, from pre-launch to end-of-life operations. Phases of conjunction assessment include launch, early orbit, on-orbit, collision avoidance, and de-orbit or disposal. Launch conjunction assessment is the process of predicting and reporting the close approaches between launch vehicles and orbiting objects. This is done by screening planned launch trajectories against all objects in the space catalog. The launch provider typically generates the trajectories, which may include multiple iterations corresponding to different launch times within the launch's window of opportunity.

The process of launch screening compares the trajectory of the launch vehicle (delivered as ephemeris data) to a catalog of space objects. The preliminary screening process may begin weeks to days ahead of the launch date depending on the launch provider's or launch range's requirements. Subsequent screenings are then performed at predetermined intervals, such as at T–4, 3, and 2 days before launch, and finally on the day of the launch, to produce the most accurate and timely assessment.

Screening results are provided for predetermined screening volumes that depend on the satellite mission. For example, a robotic mission with active payloads may use a stand-off screening distance of 25 kilometers. This means that the launch operator will be notified of any predicted close approaches with miss distances less than that.

A number of entities provide launch conjunction assessment services. The US military performs launch conjunction assessment for all launches that occur from the US Air Force's eastern and western launch ranges, as well as for any other global launch provider who requests the service. Other data providers, such as Aerospace Corporation, also provide launch conjunction assessment, and many launch agencies across the world perform independent internal assessments using publicly available data.

There is ongoing debate about the usefulness of pre-launch conjunction assessment. In many cases, there is a significant amount of uncertainty in the predicted insertion orbit and the predicted trajectories of existing satellites. As a result, launch conjunction assessments may yield a high degree of false positives, and may unnecessarily cause launch delays or aborts. Some launch operators have concluded that it is only worthwhile to conduct launch conjunction assessments against the International Space Station, while others do so for a much larger number of satellites and debris objects. However, one significant benefit of conducting launch conjunction assessment screenings is that a satellite operator will discover which other objects are "in the neighborhood," and thus which other operators they will need to establish working relationships with. In some cases, satellite operators have decided to modify the planned operational orbit for their satellite based on a launch conjunction assessment which showed that it was going into a high-traffic region. In the case of China's *TanSat*, the decision was made to not launch it into the "A-Train" constellation of Earth observation satellites due to the complicated requirements and procedures necessary for all participants in the A-Train.

Early-orbit conjunction assessment spans the phase from the spacecraft's separation from the launch vehicle to its arrival at its final orbit. This phase can take days or months depending on the maneuver plan and methods, and presents unique challenges to the conjunction assessment process. First, the limited observational data in the first few days after launch can delay the ability to generate an accurate prediction of a newly launched object's future trajectory. Additionally, the spacecraft's constant maneuvering makes it difficult to maintain consistent tracking and updated orbit determinations. Consequently, accurate and timely early-orbit conjunction assessments often require the use of operator-provided data for ephemeris-based screenings.

Early-orbit conjunction assessment typically includes the operator providing the early-orbit maneuver plan to a data provider in addition to a schedule of planned maneuvers and required screening volumes. As the early-orbit phase progresses, the operator provides ephemeris to the data provider for pre- and post-maneuver screenings against the space catalog. This data exchange allows the operator to perform collision avoidance, if needed, and helps the data provider maintain accurate positional data for the maneuvering satellite. The JSpOC provides this service to all satellite operators who provide their ephemeris, and some space agencies also provide the service for their own governmental payloads. Several private entities, including academic and commercial companies, have started to offer SSA data and services.

However, as is the case with launch conjunction assessments, early-orbit conjunctions can be difficult to predict in advance. A real life situation where early orbit conjunction assessment created challenges involved Europe's *Sentinel 1-A* satellite. *Sentinel 1-A* was launched on April 3, 2014, and within its first day on orbit, it was predicted to have a very close approach with a defunct American satellite which had not shown up during the launch screening. Planning and conducting the maneuver proved to be very challenging, as *Sentinel 1-A* was still in the process of conducting a set of maneuvers to deploy its solar arrays and antennas. Ultimately, the maneuver went smoothly and a potentially disastrous situation was avoided.

On-orbit conjunction assessment is primarily used to ensure spaceflight safety throughout the lifetime of a satellite. The process screens all active satellites against all other cataloged space objects. The results provide satellite operators with predictions of future close approach events. The close approach prediction information allows satellite operators to take actions to mitigate the risk of collision. The primary metric for doing so should be the probability of collision (Pc).

Close approach screening results are performed for prediction times that are dependent upon the satellite's orbital regime. The prediction time for satellites in GEO is typically longer than that of all other regimes, largely because GEO orbits are more predictable over long periods. The screening volume also varies across the different orbital regimes, and often includes a larger monitoring volume and a smaller high-interest, or reporting, volume. Table 7 provides an example of how different orbital regimes may be defined and assigned specific screening durations and volumes depending on their level of risk.

Examples of CA Screening Volumes					
Orbit Regime	Orbit Regime Criteria/Definition	Predict/ Propagate/ Time	Radial Miss (km)	In-Track Miss (km)	Cross-Track Miss (km)
GEO	1300min < Period < 1800 min Eccentricity < 0.25 & Inclination < 35°	10 days	12	364	30
HEO 1	Perigee < 2000 km & Eccentricity > 0.25	10 days	40	77	107
MEO	600 min < Period < 800 min Eccentricity < 0.25	10 days	2.2	17	21
LEO 4	1200 km < Perigee ≤ 2000 km Eccentricity < 0.25	7 days	0.5	2	2
LEO 3	750 km < Perigee ≤ 1200 km Eccentricity < 0.25	7 days	0.5	12	10
LEO 2	500 km < Perigee ≤ 750 km Eccentricity < 0.25	7 days	0.5	28	29
LEO 1	Perigee ≤ 500 km Eccentricity < 0.25	7 days	2	44	51

Table 7 – Examples of CA Screening Volumes

The satellite operator, data provider, or service provider may perform conjunction screenings based on schedules dictated by specific missions using any variation of trajectories, as described before. Currently, the JSpOC is the primary data provider for global space operators, and performs catalog and ephemeris screenings using their High Accuracy Catalog (HAC). The JSpOC provides catalog screenings at a minimum of once per day for all active objects, and additional ephemeris-based results when satellite operators provide state information from ephemeris files. The latter screening process is useful when satellite operators wish to screen trajectories for planned maneuvers. Service providers such as the Space Data Association specialize in ephemeris-versus-ephemeris screenings, a complementary service for satellite operators who elect to join the organization.

Conjunction assessment reports may be issued and exchanged in a variety of ways, but the prevailing standard is the Conjunction Data Message (CDM) that has been defined by the Consultative Committee for Space Data Systems (CCSDS), an international body of space agencies. Although the JSpOC is currently the premier data provider for spaceflight safety, it does not provide advanced analysis or risk mitigation recommendations. Rather, the organization provides the maximum amount of releasable data to allow operators to devise and execute their own risk mitigation strategies. Other governmental and non-governmental entities, such as NASA, the French National Center for Space Studies (CNES), and the SDA, may provide advanced analysis or recommendations to their satellite operators.

Risk Assessment and Avoiding Collisions

Not all satellites possess on-orbit maneuvering capability, but for potential collisions that involve at least one satellite with maneuvering capability, decisions on whether to conduct maneuvers to reduce the risk of a collision must be made. The decisions involve calculating the risk of collision and the potential costs of a maneuver (such as expending fuel or disrupting operations). Calculating the risk of collision requires not just knowledge of where the two objects will be, but also the amount of uncertainty associated with that knowledge. The location and uncertainty give the probability of collision, which must be future-combined with the consequences of a particular collision scenario.

Unfortunately, just calculating the probability of a collision is difficult. Most of the data that is currently publicly available on space debris and other satellites—including that provided by the JSpOC—does not include information on the uncertainty of the data, for national security reasons. Although the JSpOC has recently begun including uncertainty data in the conjunction summary messages (CSMs) it sends to satellite operators, it can be misleading due to limitations resulting from decisions made in designing the Space Surveillance Network (SSN). When the SSN was built, data storage and bandwidth were at a premium, so it was not practical to send all the observations collected during a satellite pass by a phased-array radar back for processing. Instead, the data was (and still is) sub-sampled to extract a minimal set of data—eliminating much of the associated uncertainty in the measurements. As a result, the uncertainty associated with that orbital estimate can be incorrectly interpreted as being more accurate than it actually is. The problem is further compounded when tracking maneuvering satellites, since failing to recognize that a maneuver has occurred can create a bad orbital prediction, over-inflated uncertainty, or both. Similar results can be seen when trying to process observations for GEO satellites operating in clusters when observations are incorrectly associated with the individual satellites.

From a practical perspective, it is incumbent upon each operator to do their best to track their own satellites, regularly calibrate their results against other data sources (particularly to avoid unplanned system glitches), and be willing to share that data with other operators in as timely a fashion as possible. The predicted trajectory should include natural perturbations and previously planned orbital maneuvers, and new orbital estimates should be provided as soon as possible after performing a maneuver or incorporating or canceling a planned maneuver. That data should be provided in the form of ephemerides far enough into the future to allow sharing and analysis of the data in support of decision-making—that is, early enough to plan and conduct an avoidance maneuver, if it is deemed necessary.

In the face of missing, incomplete, or potentially misleading uncertainty information, it is imperative that a variety of orbital data sources be compared

> From a practical perspective, it is incumbent upon each operator to do their best to track their own satellites, regularly calibrate their results against other data sources (particularly to avoid unplanned system glitches), and be willing to share that data with other operators in as timely a fashion as possible.

to assess a more realistic uncertainty of the relevant orbits. This process must be applied for every case—not assumed to be the same from case to case.

Although it is impossible to prevent all collisions, these steps can mitigate the probability of a serious collision that can completely disable a satellite occurring and thereby creating the next large piece of debris or generating even more small debris that jeopardizes the entire near-Earth orbital environment. Collaboration and sharing—between satellite operators and between operators and tracking services—are key to success.

Space Weather

In addition to possible collisions with other space objects, the space environment itself can also pose a hazard to satellites. "Space weather" is the term for the set of physical and electromagnetic processes and effects that occur on the sun, and ultimately interact with the Earth's magnetic sphere, atmosphere, and surface. These phenomena, which include solar flares, solar wind, geomagnetic storms, and coronal mass ejections, can have adverse effects on activities in orbit and on the Earth's surface.

The sun is constantly emitting electrically charged particles, which flow outward throughout the solar system in a phenomenon known as solar wind. The sun also emits electromagnetic radiation across a variety of wavelengths including radio, infrared, visible light, ultraviolet, and X-rays. Changes in the intensity of these emissions result in the variety of effects known as space weather events, including:

- Sunspots, which can lead to increased emission of solar wind. A geomagnetic storm results, which in mild cases leads to the aurorae borealis and australis, and in more severe cases can overload electrical systems.
- Coronal mass ejections, which correlate with increased numbers of electrically charged particles being ejected into the solar wind, and which have effects similar to those of sunspots.
- Coronal holes, which also cause increased solar wind activity.
- Solar flares, which result in high-concentration bursts of radiation.

Outside of the aurorae, space weather affects are generally not visible to the naked eye. For the most part, the Earth's natural magnetic field protects the planet from the general solar and radiation environment. However, when space weather events occur, they can have deleterious impacts on spacecraft operations that operators need to be aware of. These include:

- Higher levels than normal of charged particles, which might degrade satellite components and equipment;
- Interference with electrical signals, including those of high-frequency and ultra-high-frequency communications satellites and global navigation satellite systems (GNSS);
- Interference with radar and/or space tracking systems looking in sunward or poleward directions;
- Increased drag for satellites operating in low Earth orbit; and
- The potential for increased radiation exposure for humans in orbit.

Strong space weather events can also impact vulnerable systems on Earth's surface, including electrical power grids and aviation systems.

Space weather is typically correlated with an 11-year cycle of solar maximum and minimum, although notable events can occur at any point in the cycle. Government agencies, including the National Oceanic and Atmospheric Administration's Space Weather Prediction Center (NOAA SWPC) and the US Air Force, provide space weather forecast services, including offering watches, warnings, and alerts. Depending on the type of space weather event, warnings, watches, and alerts can be issued with between 10 minutes and 72 hours of advance notice. Space weather events are rated by a published scale to describe their expected severity. Operators and other interested parties can subscribe to the forecast service via NOAA's Space Weather Prediction Center.

Satellite Anomaly Recognition, Response, and Recovery

Anomalies in spacecraft operations come in many forms and result from a variety of causes, but are generally described as off-nominal behavior of an individual unit, a subsystem, or the system as a whole. Exact causes of anomalies can cover a broad range of sources, such as the space environment (e.g., high-energy particles from coronal mass ejections, micrometeoroid strikes, spacecraft charging), poor design (e.g., thermal runaway caused by insufficient thermal insulation, divide-by-zero cases within flight software), faulty parts or manufacturing techniques (e.g., debris in bearing races, switch failure), and even procedural or human error during operations (e.g., incorrect sequence of steps for unit power-on, accidentally transmitting unintended commands, unintentional ground- or space-based radiofrequency interference).

At one end of the spectrum, an anomaly may be benign—to the extent that it goes unnoticed for days, weeks, months, or even years. At the other extreme, an anomaly may end a mission. Properly and thoroughly preparing for, responding to, and learning from anomalies can make the difference between exceeding life expectancies for a mission and experiencing a potentially avoidable mission-ending event.

Anomaly Recognition

Several steps can be taken to improve an operator's ability to quickly detect anomalies during spacecraft operations. The most important element is having useful, accurate telemetry. All telemetry access points need clear definition of nominal and off-nominal states or operating ranges. Defining operating ranges generally takes several iterations: the first is the predicted range from unit designers, the second is based on unit test and integration data, and the third is based on initial on-orbit characterization data.

As insight into the inner workings of a system is only as good as the data available, telemetry format composition should not be overlooked. Not all parameters should be telemetered at the same rate. For example, power failure signatures have very short durations (milliseconds), while thermal signatures generally take time to manifest (seconds to tens of seconds, if not longer). Therefore, power-related data should be telemetered more frequently than thermistor.

Software components are inherently susceptible to single-event effects (SEEs) caused by energetic particles in the space environment. There is ample literature available on SEEs and methods for designing to account for and respond to them. As a starting point, integrating an error detection and correction (EDAC) capability will help reduce the impact of single-event upsets (SEUs), a type of SEE, but will not fully eliminate the risk of SEUs affecting system performance. Establishing a mechanism to routinely monitor and correct the overall state of data in on-board memory can help catch and correct issues before they manifest. In addition, telemetering the status of autonomous corrective actions (quantity, date/time, location in memory) can provide great insight into the space environment encountered as well as the health of a memory unit itself. For example, repeated attempts to correct the same memory address can provide an indication of a failed or stuck bit.

Anomaly Response

Prior to launch, operational procedures should be written, tested, and trained on in order for operators to be adequately prepared to not only perform daily operations but also respond to on-orbit failures. When developing operational procedures for anomaly response, it is helpful to define strategic decision points in the flow of steps. Consider which steps operators are authorized to execute without supervisory authority and which steps require stakeholder direction (corporate/government/customer) to perform. In defining decision points, also consider what information is necessary to choose the path forward and clearly articulate this information in objective terms. In addition, modularity in procedure design can be useful, as can expected entry/exit states and anticipated duration for the execution of each module.

For LEO systems, if manual intervention is required to respond to an anomalous condition, it must take place during one of the brief in-view periods; therefore, planning quick and concise steps with clear break-points is vital. Prior to the vehicle going out of view, it must be configured to a safe state—a state in which there is little to no risk of further damage or loss of mission until the next in-view period. Similarly, upcoming orbital events in all regimes must be considered. For response to a power system anomaly, for instance, it is important to have heightened awareness of an upcoming eclipse for which the system must be properly charged and configured. If a sufficient state of charge is not possible, a typical response would be to power off non-critical units to allow for safe transit during the eclipse period.

Once all of the above factors have been considered, a system has been built and launched, and on-orbit operations are underway, failures will inevitably happen. In a perfect world, all failure scenarios have been well-thought-out and detailed operational procedures established along with appropriate responses. In the real world, however, unforeseen and undocumented failures will happen.

When a failure occurs, anomaly response protocol takes effect. The first step in the protocol is an immediate response: any operator action or reliance on autonomous fault sequence required to configure the vehicle to a "safe" state. The second step is to initiate a call-in procedure to alert and request assistance and support from management and system or subsystem experts, based on observed signature. The third step is establishing authority for action: defining who is in charge of response and recovery actions, which may be the operational crew, factory experts, the owner of the system, or others. The final step is communicating the impact of the anomaly: determining what the immediate effect is on the mission, the duration of the projected outage/impact, and who needs to be informed.

Once a vehicle has been "safed" (configured in a known state it can stay in more or less indefinitely without concern, disregarding a second, unrelated anomaly), operators can begin compiling information about the failure while system experts arrive. Useful information includes a detailed timeline of events leading up to the anomaly, detailed state of all systems on the vehicle before and after the fault, and a timeline of upcoming events such as out-of-view periods, an eclipse, or conjunctions.

Anomaly Recovery and Analysis

An anomaly response team should consist of general vehicle system engineers familiar with the detailed workings of the system as a whole, subsystem and unit specialists educated on specific hardware and software intricacies of the various units, and representatives of the stakeholders or customers. While all satellite operations groups have their own processes for anomaly response, recovery, and investigation, an anomaly recovery usually begins with vehicle system engineers piecing together details of the scenario and working with individual subsystem specialists to identify abnormal behavior in all aspects of a system, both prior to and following the fault. Due to the complexity of space systems and wide variety of potential causes, a specific root cause many times cannot be attributed on the day of an anomaly. Rather, suspect units are isolated and kept offline until further investigation can take place. In cases where redundant units are available, full operations may be re-established by performing a controlled swap to a redundant unit, if not already performed by on-board fault management.

In general, there are two main severities of anomalies: critical and payload-related. Critical health and safety anomalies affect communications, power, and thermal or attitude control subsystems, and payload-related anomalies may affect execution of the intended mission but do not necessarily affect the ability of the vehicle to control its subsystems. For vehicle health and safety anomalies, autonomous fault management response should be designed and tested to quickly establish safe control of the affected systems. In these cases, the anomaly response team should focus initial efforts on confirming that autonomous commanding successfully identified the fault, executed the proper response sequence, and isolated the suspect unit(s). For non-critical but mission-impacting anomalies, the anomaly team should focus efforts on isolating the fault and investigating the best path forward to re-establishing mission throughput, perhaps on redundant units or in a degraded state if redundant units are not available.

At a point in the anomaly response and recovery process, a full root cause analysis should take place. However, in practice, it is very rarely possible to determine a single definitive root cause. More often, the diagram and paths are narrowed to several "probable root causes" and several "unlikely root causes," and the remainder are "exonerated." Due to the challenges associated with remotely identifying component-level failures from hundreds to millions of miles away with limited insight, many root cause investigations remain open, documented with probable but not definitive causes.

Fishbone Diagrams

Fishbone diagrams provide a clear and concise way to visually track investigations that have a multitude of potential root causes (Figure 9). "Bones" on the fishbone diagram typically include, at minimum:

- Environmental causes (e.g., space weather, debris, etc.),
- Design/parts/manufacturing causes (down to each piece-part within the failure path), and
- Human/operator causes. As aspects are vetted and eliminated, bones on the fishbone chart can be exonerated. The goal of a deep-dive root cause analysis is to narrow a fishbone diagram down to a single bone that can be deemed the "determined root cause."

Regardless of the absolute determination of the root cause, lessons are always learned from anomalies, lessons which can be applied to the current mission as well as others in a constellation and even across the industry. For example, failure

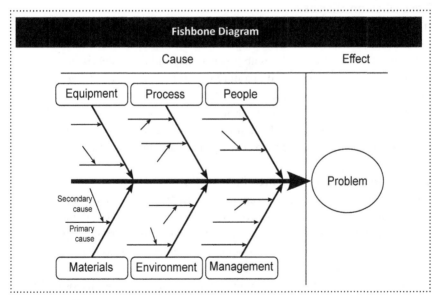

Figure 9 – Fishbone Diagram
Source: https//commons.wikimedia.org

of the bearings in a reaction wheel on a LEO vehicle due to lube breakdown may provide early warning of potential trouble with control moment gyros built by the same vendor and used on a different vehicle in a different orbital regime. Therefore, documenting, cataloging, and maintaining failure information is paramount to the success of any space program, as is sharing lessons learned within the space operations community.

Ultimately, it is important to accept that on-orbit anomalies will happen over the lifetime of a space vehicle. Being adequately prepared before anomalies occur and applying lessons learned afterwards can drastically reduce the impacts to mission throughput.

END-OF-LIFE

As satellites reach their end of life and cessation of operations, it is important for satellite operators to dispose of satellites properly. Highly used and important regions of orbit are already congested, in large part due to satellites or rocket stages that have been left in those active regions. Increasingly, there are national regulatory obligations, contractual obligations, guarantees, and other responsibilities that need to be met during the end-of-life phase of a space mission.

Post-Mission Disposal

It is important to properly dispose of satellites and launch vehicles at the end of useable life. Satellites that are not properly disposed of have a chance of interfering with operating satellites and possibly generating additional debris in orbits that are useful and commonly used. To minimize this risk, the Inter-Agency Space Debris Coordination Committee (IADC), an international governmental forum of experts, has created guidelines for mission developers to use when planning proper disposal of spacecraft. In addition, thirteen nations are participating in an effort organized within the ISO to develop space systems disposal standards.

Launch Vehicle and Satellite Passivation

To minimize the risk of satellites creating debris from accidental break-ups after the completion of mission operations, the IADC recommends that all the on-board sources of stored energy of a spacecraft or launch-vehicle orbital stage, such as residual propellants, batteries, high-pressure vessels, self-destructive devices, and flywheels and momentum wheels, should be depleted or safed when they are no longer required for mission operations or post-mission disposal. This is called passivation.

The importance of designing for proper passivation has been demonstrated by the more than 40 ullage motors flown on the Russian *Proton Block DM* upper stage that have broken up in orbit. The ullage motors, first deployed in the 1980s, provide the stage with three-axis control during coast, and are routinely ejected when the *Block DM* stage ignites for the final time. Depending on the mission profile, the ullage motors may carry up to 40 kilograms of unused propellant. Over time, solar heating and other factors have caused dozens of the motors to explode, releasing debris into orbit. Russia has made design changes to prevent accidental explosion of the engines on new *Block DM* models, but some launches continue to eject the units.

International Orbital Debris Limitation Documents	
Entity	**Document**
IADC	IADC-02-01, Rev 1
ISO	ISO 26872, ISO 16699, ISO 16164
USA	US Government Orbital Debris Mitigation Standard Practices
NASA	NPR 8715.6A, NASA-STD-8719.14
Department of Defense (DoD)	DoD Space Policy Directive, 3100.10, AFI 91-217
FAA	Title 14, Code of Federal Regulations (CFR) Part 415.39
JAXA	JAXA JMR-003
CNES	MPM-50-00-12
European Space Agency (ESA)	European Code of Conduct for Space Debris Mitigation
Roscosmos	Space Technology Items General Requirements on Mitigation of Space Debris Population

Table 8 – International Orbital Debris Limitation Documents

According to the IADC guidelines, passivation should occur as soon as the process can be undertaken without posing unacceptable risk to the satellite payload. Guidelines include the following:

- Residual propellants and other fluids, such as pressurants, should be depleted as thoroughly as possible, either by depletion burns or venting, to prevent accidental break-ups caused by over-pressurization or chemical reaction.

| 125

- Batteries should be adequately designed and manufactured, both structurally and electrically, to prevent break-ups. Pressure increase in battery cells and assemblies can be prevented by mechanical measures unless these measures cause an excessive reduction of mission assurance. At the end of operations, battery charging lines should be de-activated.
- High-pressure vessels should be vented to a level guaranteeing that no break-ups can occur. Leak-before-burst designs are beneficial but are not sufficient to meet all passivation recommendations of propulsion and pressurization systems. Heat pipes may be left pressurized if the probability of rupture can be demonstrated to be very low.
- Self-destruct systems should be designed to not cause unintentional destruction due to inadvertent commands, thermal heating, or RF interference.
- Power to flywheels and momentum wheels should be terminated during the disposal phase.
- Other forms of stored energy should be assessed and adequate mitigation measures should be applied.
- Telemetry and other forms of RF from the satellite should be turned off.
- All communications should be disabled.

Geosynchronous Region Disposal

The geosynchronous region is a special area of Earth orbit. This is defined as 200 kilometers above and below the geostationary altitude of 35,786 kilometers and 15 degrees north and south of the Equator. Maintaining a spacecraft in GEO in the geosynchronous region requires expenditure of fuel over time to maintain a fixed position in space relative to Earth. GEO satellites are disposed of by maneuvering the spacecraft further out into space, away from the protected geosynchrous region. However, the decision on when to retire a GEO satellite can be a difficult tradeoff.

GEO satellites often face depletion of fuel before other satellite subsystems reach end-of-life. Therefore, operators often must make the difficult decision to retire a satellite that is generating tens of millions of dollars annually, when the only thing wrong with it is its low fuel. The lifespan tradeoff is made more difficult because satellite operators, using newly available low-cost tracking user terminals, can choose to conduct operations from an inclined orbit. In an inclined orbit, fuel is expended at a much reduced rate as the satellite is allowed to drift within a certain region of space, allowing it to continue to be useful. However, there is a risk that other satellite subsystems, operating beyond their design life, may fail during inclined operations, leaving the satellite in an orbit that risks contaminating the protected geosynchronous region.

The IADC recommends fulfilling the two following conditions at the end of the disposal phase to describe an orbit that remains above the geosynchronous protected region:

1. A minimum increase in perigee altitude of:
   235 km + (1000 × CR × A/m)
   where CR is   the solar radiation pressure coefficient
   A/m is   the aspect area to dry mass ratio (m2kg-1)
   235 km is   the sum of the upper altitude of the GSO
                      protected region (200 km) and the maximum descent
                      of a re-orbited spacecraft due to luni-solar &
                      geopotential perturbations (35 km)
2. An eccentricity less than or equal to 0.003

To minimize the chance of debris-creation, a propulsion system should not be separated from a GEO spacecraft. In the event that there are unavoidable reasons that require separation, the propulsion system should be designed to be left in an orbit that is, and will remain, outside of the protected geosynchronous region. Regardless of whether it is separated or not, a propulsion system should be designed for passivation. In addition, spacecraft operators should design missions to avoid leaving launch vehicle orbital stages in the geosynchronous region. Most GEO operators require that manufacturers design for one more year than required for operation so that the satellite can be moved above the geostationary orbit and allowed to drift away into deep space.

Passing Through LEO Disposal

Some types of launches leave rocket bodies or other fragments in orbits that pass through LEO. Often this is the case with launches to place a GEO satellite into a geostationary transfer orbit (GTO), a navigation satellite in medium Earth orbit (MEO), or a satellite in highly elliptical Molniya orbits. Whenever possible, spacecraft or orbital stages that are terminating their operational phases in orbits that pass through the LEO region, or have the potential to interfere with the LEO region, should be de-orbited (direct re-entry is preferred), or, where appropriate, maneuvered into an orbit with a reduced lifetime. Retrieval is also a disposal option.

According to the IADC, a spacecraft or orbital stage should be left in an orbit in which, using an accepted nominal projection for solar activity, atmospheric drag will limit the orbital lifetime after completion of operations to 25 years. If a spacecraft or orbital stage is to be disposed of by re-entry into the atmosphere, debris that survives to reach the surface of the Earth should not pose an undue risk to people or property. To minimize the risk of debris surviving re-entry, it is advisable to design a satellite in a manner that results in complete vaporization during re-entry. If that is not possible and there is a greater than 1 in 10,000 chance of causing a fatality, it is necessary to perform a controlled re-entry that deposits surviving debris into uninhabited regions, such as broad ocean areas. In addition, ground environmental pollution, caused by radioactive substances, toxic substances, or any other environmental pollutants resulting from on-board articles, should be prevented or minimized in order to be accepted as permissible.

In the event of a controlled re-entry of a spacecraft or orbital stage, the operator of the system should inform the relevant air traffic and maritime traffic authorities of the re-entry time and trajectory and the associated ground area.

Atmospheric Re-Entry and Risk Assessment

Spacecraft designers must consider what will happen to a spacecraft at the end of its lifespan. For satellites operating in LEO, it is likely that atmospheric drag will eventually cause a spacecraft to re-enter Earth's atmosphere. As satellites re-enter, they disintegrate, but some debris may survive the heat of re-entry and could impact the ground and cause casualties. Unfortunately, it is very difficult to predict specifically where debris will impact as the density of the Earth's atmosphere is constantly changing. It is recommended that satellite operators design spacecraft that will completely burn up during re-entry.

If debris is expected to survive re-entry and cause an unacceptable risk of casualties, it is

If debris is expected to survive re-entry and cause an unacceptable risk of casualties, it is necessary for mission planners to conduct a controlled re-entry that will spread debris over uninhabited areas of the Earth's surface.

necessary for mission planners to conduct a controlled re-entry that will spread debris over uninhabited areas of the Earth's surface.

Re-Entry

During re-entry, friction and compression generate immense heat as a satellite traveling more than 29,000 kilometers per hour enters the atmosphere. That tremendous heat can melt and vaporize the entire spacecraft. However, if a satellite component's melting temperature is not reached during re-entry then that object can survive re-entry and impact the ground. In addition to heat and pressure, a spacecraft experiences immense loads as it decelerates. These loads, which can exceed 10 Gs, or ten times the acceleration of gravity at the Earth's surface, coupled with the immense heat, cause a spacecraft's structure to break apart. The broken-up components will continue to decelerate and, depending on the density of the atmosphere in the region of re-entry, may reach a low ground speed, virtually falling straight down from the sky. The broken-up spacecraft should impact the ground at relatively low speeds, but it still presents a hazard to people and property on the ground and a satellite operator will be liable for damages caused by the debris.

End-of-Life Disposal Actions				
Disposal Action	Subsynchronous GTO	Supersynchronous GTO	MEO Navigation Satellite Orbits	Molniya
25-Year Decay	Lower perigee to ~ 200 km	Initial perigee ~ 200 km	Not recommended due to large Delta-V (DV) or change in velocity required	Not studied, but lowering perigee would require least DV
Disposal Orbit	Between 2500 km and GEO-500 km. Launch Vehicle Upper Stages should reach GEO-500 km in less than 25 years.	Not recommended	TBC: 1. Minimum long-term perigee of 2000 km, apogee below MEO. 2. Perigee 500 km above MEO or nearby operational region and e < 0.003; RAAN and argument of perigee selected for stability	Set initial perigee of disposal orbit at 3000 km
Direct Reentry	Broad ocean area impact or other safe zone	Not studied, but similar to Sub-synchronous GTO case	Not recommended due to large DV required	Broad ocean area impact or other safe zone

Table 9 – End-of-Life Disposal Actions

Predicting the exact area where debris will impact from a random re-entering satellite is difficult because drag on the object is directly proportional to atmospheric density, and the density of the atmosphere varies greatly at high altitudes and is affected—dramatically even—by solar activity. It is possible to predict the time a re-entry will begin within a 10 percent margin of the actual time. However, a minute of error in time is equivalent to hundreds of miles of area because of the great speeds of re-entering objects.

About 10 to 40 percent of a satellite's mass will survive re-entry, depending on the size, shape, weight, and material composition. The area it will strike is called a footprint. It is possible to predict the size of a footprint but very difficult to determine specifically where the debris footprint will be located on the Earth's surface. The size of the footprint is determined by estimating the breakup altitude of the satellite or space hardware and then modeling the mass and aerodynamic properties of surviving debris. Footprint lengths vary in size from approximately 185 kilometers to 2,000 kilometers, depending on the complexity and characteristics of the object. The width of a footprint can be affected by winds, with the greatest uncertainty affecting the lightest objects. A 20- to 40-kilometer footprint width is typical.

Re-Entry Threat Statistics

While the impact threat to human life and property from re-entry debris is serious, it is interesting to note that only one person has ever claimed to have been struck by falling space debris, and that person was hit by a lightweight object and was not injured. Over the last 50 years, more than 5,400 metric tons of material are believed to have survived re-entry, but no casualties from the debris have been reported. It has even been calculated that the risk that an individual will be struck by re-entered debris is less than 1 in 1 trillion.

Calculating Re-Entry Risk

There is no legal international definition of "unacceptable safety risk" for re-entry. The United Nations space debris mitigation guidelines leave the definition of acceptable risk to national authorities. The IADC identifies two guidelines to follow. First, to minimize the accumulation of orbital debris, it recommends satellite missions leave a satellite in an orbit that will result in re-entry within 25 years. About 80 percent of rocket upper-stages currently comply with the rule, while only 60 percent of satellites are designed to lower their orbits to re-enter within 25 years. While compliance is not perfect, most major spacefaring nations support the 25-year rule and are taking steps to improve compliance.

In addition to the 25-year rule, the IADC recommends that if a satellite has a 1 in 10,000 chance of surviving re-entry and causing a casualty, its re-entry must be controlled. For a piece of debris that survives atmospheric re-entry, the debris casualty area is the average debris cross-sectional area plus a factor for the cross-section of a standing individual. The total debris casualty area for a re-entry event is the sum of the debris casualty areas for all debris pieces that survive atmospheric re-entry. The total human casualty expectation is equal to the total casualty debris area times the average population density for the particular orbit. A variety of models exist to calculate the likelihood that specific pieces of a satellite will survive re-entry, including NASA's Debris Assessment Software or its higher-fidelity Object Re-entry Survival Analysis Tool.

Design for Demise

Design for Demise is a method of satellite design with the goal of ensuring each component of a satellite will be completely destroyed during the heat of re-entry. By designing for demise, satellite operators can avoid having to conduct a controlled re-entry, which can lengthen the mission lifespan, lower the cost of development, and reduce the mission ground-support costs. Design for Demise is a great approach for ensuring compliance with the 1 in 10,000 risk threshold. The International Organization for Standardization (ISO) is developing standards (ISO 27875:2010) that can be applied at the planning, design, and review stages of satellite development to assess, reduce, and control the potential risk that spacecraft and launch-vehicle orbital stage pose during re-entry.

Re-Entry Predictions

Spacecraft re-entries are tracked by space surveillance systems around the globe. The US Space Surveillance Network is the largest system, and uses radar and optical sensors at various sites around the world to track objects in space. The SSN sensors can be used to determine a re-entry object's orbit. This tracking information, along with data about changing atmospheric density, is used to predict atmospheric re-entries. USSTRATCOM shares satellite tracking information with other nations and the private satellite operators through its Satellite Catalogue and the publicly available website **www.space-track.org**. USSTRATCOM issues Tracking and Impact Prediction messages at intervals including T–4 days, T–3 days, T–2 days, T–1 day, T–12 hours, T–6 hours, and T–2 hours. Re-entry predictions must be continually updated as a satellite approaches the atmosphere.

Even predictions made within a few hours of re-entry may project a debris footprint that is incorrect by hundreds to thousands of kilometers. Therefore, even if a significant amount of debris is expected to survive re-entry, it is not logistically plausible to effectively evacuate areas debris might impact.

Planning a Controlled Re-Entry

If significant portions of a satellite are expected to survive re-entry and violate the 1 in 10,000 chance casualty threshold, it is important for a satellite designer to plan a controlled re-entry that will scatter any remaining debris over an unpopulated part of the ocean. A controlled re-entry requires a satellite maneuvering strategy that avoids possible collision with space debris or other satellites. Adequate fuel must be left in a satellite's tanks to perform the final orbit-changing burns. Ground support teams must be available to coordinate, perform, and monitor the final satellite maneuvers.

INDEX

A

active debris removal (ADR), 35,37
anomalies, 94, 100, 119-120, 122-124
  fishbone diagram, 123
  links between testing and, 100
  mitigation, 100
  recognition, response, and recovery, 119
arbitration, 30, 82-83
Argentina, 72-73
Asia-Pacific Regional Space Agency Forum
(APRSAF), 62
  Asia-Pacific Satellite Communications
  Council (APSCC), 50
asteroid mining, *see* space resources
astronauts, 41
  Astronaut Agreement, 6, 7, 42
  envoys of mankind, 41
atmospheric re-entry, *see* re-entry
Australia, 73, 74, 75
Austria, 49, 73

B

batch processor, 110-111
Belarus, 73
Belgium, 73
Bogotá Declaration, 39
Bolivia, 62
boundary between airspace and outer space,
  see delimitation
Brazil, 73, 74, 75

C

Canada, 73, 76
  Remote Sensing Space Systems Act, 85
Catapult, *see* United Kingdom (UK), Case Study
  - Satellite Applications Catapult
Chile, 73, 86
  space policy, 62
China, 24, 49, 62, 73, 77, 114
  Tansat, 114
CNES, *see* France, space agency
Colombia, 39
Commercial Spaceflight Federation (CSF), 50

Committee on the Peaceful Uses of
  Outer Space (COPUOS), *see* United Nations
  (UN), Committee on the Peaceful Uses of
  Outer Space
Conference on Disarmament,
  see United Nations (UN),
  Conference on Disarmament (CD)
Conjunction Assessment (CA), 111-116
  risk assessment, 116-119
Consultative Committee for
  Space Data Systems (CCSDS), 24, 116
contract types, 82
  cost reimbursement, 82
  fixed price, 82
  time and materials, 82
Copernicus, *see* European Space Agency (ESA),
  Copernicus
coronal holes, *see* space weather
Coronal Mass Ejection (CME),
  see space weather
COSPAR, *see* International Committee on
  Space Research (COSPAR)
cost reimbursement, *see* contract types
Czech Republic, 73

D

debris mitigation, *see* space debris
delimitation, 38-40
  functionalist approach, 39
  Kármán line, 39
  spatialist approach, 39
design for demise, 131
dispute settlement, 29, 81-83
Directorate of Defense Trade Controls, *see*
  United States, Directorate of Defense Trade
  Controls (DDTC)
DLR, *see* Germany, Aerospace Center

E

Earth environment, 31
Earth observation, 21-22, 74, 61, 84, 87, 114,
  see also remote sensing

national registration of space objects, 10-16
  58, 71-73
national space policy, *see* space policy,
  national policy
Netherlands, 30, 72, 73
nodal period, 11, 13
North Korea, 73
Norway, 73
Notices to Airmen (NOTAM), 104
nuclear power sources, 32-33
Nuclear Test Ban Treaty, 8

O
on-orbit activities, 107-124
Open Geospatial Consortium (OGC), 25, 52
Optional Rules for Arbitration of Disputes
  Relation to Outer Space Activities, 30, 82-83
orbit determination,
  see space situational awareness (SSA)
orbit propagation,
  see space situational awareness (SSA)
orbital parameters, 11, 13-14, 33, 85
Outer Space Treaty, 3-17
  Article I, 4-6, 10
  Article II, 38, 45-47, 69-70, 72
  Article III, 7, 8-9, 32, 70
  Article IV, 8, *see* also export control and
    technology transfer
  Article V, 41-42
  Article VI, 9-10, 27-28, 32
  Article VII, 27-28, 29, 31, 32
  Article VIII, 12, 16, 71
  Article IX, 29, 31-32, 42-45
  envoys of mankind, 41-42
  interpreting, 5-6
  liability, *see* liability
  preamble, 5
  province of all mankind, 5, 45
  state responsibility, 3, 9-10
  states parties to, 6-7, 73

P
Pakistan, 73
payload testing, 98-100
peaceful purposes, 8-9
Permanent Court of Arbitration (PCA), 30, 82

Peru, 73
planetary protection, *see* International
  Committee on Space Research (COSPAR)
preflight operations, *see* launch
primary data, *see* remote sensing
primary services, *see* International
  Telecommunication Union (ITU)
private sector, 56, 59, 63, 64-68, 79
processed data, *see* remote sensing
*Proton Block DM, see Russia, Proton
  Block DM*
province of all mankind, *see* Outer
  Space Treaty
public-private partnership, 65-66

Q

R
Radio Regulations, *see* International
  Telecommunication Union (ITU)
radioisotope heat unit (RHU), 32
radioisotope thermoelectric generator (RTG),
  32
range safety, 104-105, 106
raw data, *see* remote sensing
re-entry, 127-132
  atmospheric, 128
  cataloging risks, 130-131
  defined, 128-130
  design for demise, 131
  licenses, 91-92
  planning a controlled, 132
  predictions, 131-132
  threat statistics, 130
Registration Convention, 71-73
  Article I, 27
  Article III, 11
  Article IV, 11
  international registration, 7, 13-16
  national registries, 71-73
  states parties to, 7, 11, 71-73
REACH, *see* European Union (EU), Registration,
  Evaluation, Authorisation and Restriction of
  Chemicals (REACH)
remote sensing, 21-22

LIST OF ABBREVIATIONS

ADR	Active Debris Removal
AEB	Brazilian Space Agency
APRSAF	Asia-Pacific Regional Space Agency Forum
APSCC	Asia-Pacific Satellite Communications Council
ASI	Italian Space Agency
BELSPO	Belgian Science Policy Office
BSS	Broadcasting Satellite Services
CA	Conjunction Assessment
CCL	Commercial Control List (USA)
CCSDS	Consultative Committee for Space Data Systems
CD	Conference on Disarmament (UN)
CDM	Conjunction Data Message
CFR	Code of Federal Regulations (USA)
CNES	National Center for Space Studies (France)
CNSA	China National Space Administration
CONAE	National Commission on Space Activities of Argentina
CONIDA	National Aerospace Research and Development Center (Peru)
COPUOS	Committee on the Peaceful Uses of Outer Space (UN)
CSA	Canadian Space Agency
CSF	Commercial Spaceflight Federation
COSPAR	International Committee on Space Research
DDTC	Directorate of Defense Trade Controls (USA)
DLR	German Aerospace Center
DoD	Department of Defense (USA)
DV	Change in Velocity
EARSC	European Association of Remote Sensing Companies
EDAC	Error Detection and Connection
ESA	European Space Agency
ESOA	European, Middle East, and Africa Satellite Operators Association
EU	European Union
EUMETSAT	European Organisation for the Exploitation of Meteorological Satellites
FAA	Federal Aviation Administration (USA)
FCC	Federal Communications Commission (USA)
FMEA	Failure Modes and Effects Analysis
FSS	Fixed Satellite Services
GEO	Geostationary Earth Orbit
GEO	Group on Earth Observations
GNSS	Global Navigation Satellite Systems

GPS	Global Positioning System
GTO	Geosynchronous Transfer Orbit
HAC	High Accuracy Catalog
HEO	High Earth Orbit
I&T	Integration and Test
IAC	International Astronautical Congress
IADC	Inter-Agency Space Debris Coordination Committee
IAF	International Astronautical Federation
IARU	International Amateur Radio Union
ICAO	International Civil Aviation Organization
ICG	International Committee on Global Navigation Satellite Systems
ICJ	International Court of Justice
IISL	International Institute of Space Law
IOT	Internet of Things
ISO	International Organization for Standardization
ITAR	International Traffic in Arms Regulations (USA)
ITU	International Telecommunication Union
ITU-R	International Telecommunication Union Radiocommunication
ITU-T	International Telecommunication Union Telecommunication Standardization Sector
JAXA	Japan Aerospace Exploration Agency
JSpOC	Joint Space Operations Center (USA)
KazCosmos	Ministry for Investment and Development–Aerospace Committee (Kazakhstan)
LBA	Federal Aviation Office (Germany)
LEO	Low Earth Orbit
LSC	Legal Subcomittee (COPUOS, UN)
MEO	Medium Earth Orbit
MEXT	Ministry of Education, Sports, Culture, Science and Technology (Japan)
MIFR	Master International Frequency Register
MSIP	Ministry of Science, Information and Communications Technology, and Future Planning (South Korea)
MSS	Mobile Satellite Services
MTCR	Missile Technology Control Regime
NASA	National Aeronautics and Space Administration (USA)
NASB	National Academy of Sciences (Belarus)
NGO	Non-governmental Organization
NOAA	National Oceanic and Atmospheric Administration (USA)
NOTAMs	Notices to Airmen

NSAU	National Space Agency of Ukraine
NSC	Norwegian Space Center
NTIA	National Telecommunications and Information Administration
OD	Orbit Determination
Ofcom	Office of Communications (UK)
OGC	Open Geospatial Consortium
OOSA	Office for Outer Space Affairs (UN)
OST	Outer Space Treaty
PAROS	Prevention of an Arms Race in Outer Space
Pc	Probability of Collision
PCA	Permanent Court of Arbitration
PNG	Position, Navigation, Timing
R&D	Research and Development
RAAN	Right Ascension of the Ascending Node
REACH	Registration, Evaluation, Authorisation and Restriction of Chemicals (EU)
RF	Radiofrequency
REG	Registration Convention
RHUs	Radioisotope Heat Units
Roscosmos	State Space Corporation (Russia)
RTGs	Radioisotope Thermoelectric Generators
SDA	Space Data Association
SEEs	Single Event Effects
SEUs	Single Event Upsets
SFCG	Space Frequency Coordination Group
SIA	Satellite Industry Association
SLR	Satellite Laser Ranging
SME	Small and Medium Sized
SSA	Space Situational Awareness
SSN	Space Surveillance Network (USA)
STEM	Science, Technology, Engineering, and Mathematics
STI	Science, Technology, and Innovation
STM	Space Traffic Management
STSC	Scientific and Technical Subcommittee (COPUOS, UN)
SUPARCO	Pakistan Space and Upper Atmosphere Research Commission
SWPC	Space Weather Prediction Center (NOAA, USA)
TBC	To Be Considered
TBD	To Be Determined
TCBM	Transparency and Confidence-Building Measure

TRL	Technology Readiness Level
UAE	United Arab Emirates
UAS	Uninhabited Aircraft Systems
UK	United Kingdom
UKSA	UK Space Agency
UN	United Nations
UNCITRAL	United Nations Commission on International Trade Law
UNESCO	United Nations Educational, Scientific and Cultural Organization
UNGA	United Nations General Assembly
UN-GGIM	United Nations Committee of Experts on Global Geospatial Information Management
UN-SPIDER	United Nations Platform for Space-based Information for Disaster Management and Emergency Response
US	United States
USGS	United States Geological Survey
USML	United States Munitions List
USSR	Union of Soviet Socialist Republics
USSTRATCOM	United States Strategic Command
UTC	Coordinated Universal Time
WMO	World Meteorological Organization
WRC	World Radiocommunication Conference
WTSA	World Telecommunication Standardization Assembly